"Close protection is defined as the provision of armed or unarmed specialists to protect a nominated principal from harm."
Excerpt from a Standing Committee on Army Organisation by the Director of Military Operations, dated 30 November 1979.

This incredible work has been authored by the former Training Warrant Officer of the Royal Military Police (RMP) Close Protection Unit (CPU), Richard Keightley. Drawing upon extensive material, most of which has never been published before, Keightley chronicles the history of RMP Close Protection from its origins during the Second World War, through to current operations around the globe. It is a fascinating read that is as eye-opening as it is compelling. Although the forerunners of the RMP, as Military Mounted Police, Military Foot Police, Corps of Military Police and latterly the RMP, have always held responsibility for escorting senior commanders in operational theatres, and Her Majesty's Ambassadors and High Commissioners in high risk appointments abroad, it was not until the nineteen eighties that the RMP officially became the lead authority on Close Protection within the British Armed forces.

Today, members of the RMP, Royal Marine Police Troop and Royal Air Force Police are deployed all around the world protecting VIPs from harm; be it the drug cartels in South America, Al Qaeda in Africa or the Taliban in Afghanistan. Whether the threat against a VIP is posed by a terrorist or criminal, the level of protection provided by the Military Police remains one of professionalism, dedication and unquestionable loyalty towards the Principal. Keightley's narrative details the discipline of Close Protection and VIP work and in doing so, strips away the mysticism to reveal the intricacies - namely relentless training, attention to detail and a high tempo of operations in the complex world of modern security.

From the Northern Ireland experience through to the British Army of the Rhine (BAOR); Joint Operations and the establishment of the Close Protection Unit; training and operations including Bosnia, Iraq and Afghanistan – Keightley's vivid narrative fascinates as it illustrates the vast skill set possessed by the Red Caps of Close Protection. The wherewithal of Walking Drills, Security Advance Parties (SAPs), Residence Security Teams, (RSTs), and 'quick draws' are revealed - as are relationships with agencies such as the SAS, the Police and the Foreign & Commonwealth Office.

Some of the operational incidents make for harrowing reading but through Keightley's work, the reader is shown how training and professionalism enabled the Close Protection operatives to survive car bombs, shootings and more. 'By Example Shall We Lead' is the RMP motto and *Deter, Suppress, Extract!* shows exactly why…

Read it and be inspired. There's no one finer than the men and women of the RMP's Close Protection Unit.

Warrant Officer Class 1 Richard Keightley was born in Reading, Berkshire and after education followed his grandfather and father into the British Army, enlisting in 1986 at Oxford. Following a year at the Junior Leaders Regiment Royal Armoured Corp in Bovington, Richard finished training with the Royal Military Police at Roussillon Barracks, Chichester in June 1987. He saw postings both at home and abroad and in 1992 he attended Close Protection Course Number 61 at Longmoor before joining the staff at the Operations Wing in Kimberley House. Although Richard has revisited General Police Duties on a regular basis, his Close Protection career has seen him deploy to Northern Ireland as the Brigade Commander's bodyguard as well as Algeria, Lebanon, Burundi, Uganda, Rwanda, Iraq and Sudan in support of the Foreign and Commonwealth Office. Later in his career he saw a further tour of Iraq as Close Protection Team Leader to the Deputy Commanding General in Baghdad as well as a tour in Afghanistan as Team Leader for the NATO Ambassador, a Four Star appointment. Richard spent six years at the Close Protection Unit before being appointed RSM at 158 Pro Coy RMP in Bulford in January 2012. Richard is married to Jenny and has a son, Connor.

DETER SUPPRESS EXTRACT!

ROYAL MILITARY POLICE CLOSE PROTECTION, THE AUTHORISED HISTORY

Helion & Company

G G Books UK

Co-published in 2014 by:

Helion & Company Limited
26 Willow Road
Solihull
West Midlands
B91 1UE
England
Tel. 0121 705 3393
Fax 0121 711 4075
Email: info@helion.co.uk
Website: www.helion.co.uk

and

GG Books UK
Rugby
Warwickshire
Tel. 07921 709307
Website: www.30degreessouth.co.uk

Designed and typeset by Farr out Publications, Wokingham, Berkshire
Cover designed by Euan Carter, Leicester (www.euancarter.com)
Printed by Henry Ling Limited, Dorchester, Dorset

Text © Richard Keightley 2014
Photographs © mixture of Author, Crown Copyright and individuals named in the acknowledgements. The author would be pleased to supply further details on request, c/o publishers.

ISBN 978-1-910294-02-4

British Library Cataloguing-in-Publication Data.
A catalogue record for this book is available from the British Library.

All rights reserved. No part of this publication may be reproduced, stored in a retrieval system, or transmitted, in any form, or by any means, electronic, mechanical, photocopying, recording or otherwise, without the express written consent of Helion & Company Limited and GG Books.

For details of other military history titles published by Helion & Company Limited contact the above address, or visit our website: http://www.helion.co.uk.

We always welcome receiving book proposals from prospective authors.

This short history is dedicated to my wife, Jenny, my son, Connor, to all those who have contributed towards its production; Sgt Chris Gowler RMP, a fine role model, my Editor-in-Chief and director of the RMP Museum, Col Jeremy Green OBE and not forgetting Lt Col 'Boots' Wellington MBE RMP, who, six years ago, asked if I "could wrap it up in a couple of weeks".

Thank you all

"... close protection is defined as the provision of armed or unarmed specialists to protect a nominated principal from harm."

Excerpt from a Standing Committee on Army Organisation by the Director of Military Operations for out of Committee clearance by the Executive Committee of the Army Board, dated 30 November 1979

Contents

List of abbreviations	viii
A Principal's View by The Right Honourable The Lord Ashdown of Norton-sub-Hamdon GCMG, KBE, PC	xii
Foreword by General Sir Nick Parker KCB CBE Former Commander Land Forces	xiv
Preface	xv
Acknowledgements	xvii
1. The Early Years	22
2. 177 (Support) Pl Northern Ireland (OP BANNER)	57
3. British Army of the Rhine (BAOR), RTW Werl and UK	82
4. Early Training in the UK and 'Block 30'	91
5. Supporting the Foreign and Commonwealth Office (FCO)	95
6. Military Campaigns Post 1970	157
7. Joint Operations	166
8. Close Protection Unit Royal Military Police	173
9. Training Today	176
10. The 'Protegimus'	184
11. The Team Photograph	186
12. Behind the Scenes	191
13. A CP Operator Always Looks Out	197
Epilogue	212
Appendices	
I The Protegimus Grace	213
II Appointments, Honours and Awards	214
Bibliography	218

List of abbreviations

ADC	Aide de Camp
APM	Assistant Provost Marshal
ARRC	Allied Rapid Reaction Corps
BAOR	British Army of the Rhine
BBC	British Broadcasting Corporation
Bde	Brigade
Bde Comd	Brigade Commander
BEM	British Empire Medal
BG	Bodyguard
Brig	Brigadier
CAT	Counter-Attack Team
Capt	Captain
CBE	Commander of the Most Excellent Order of the British Empire
CinC	Commander in Chief
CLF	Commander Land Forces
CMP	Corps of Military Police
Col	Colonel
Coy	Company
Cpl	Corporal
CP	Close Protection
CPT(G)	Close Protection Team (Germany)
CPTW	Close Protection Training Wing
CPU	Close Protection Unit
CSM	Company Sergeant Major
Div	Division
DMO	Director Military Operations
DPM	Deputy Provost Marshal
DS	Directing Staff
DSACEUR	Deputy Supreme Allied Commander Europe
DSO	Distinguished Service Order
ECAB	Executive Committee of the Army Board

LIST OF ABBREVIATIONS

EOKA	Ethniki Organosis Kyprion Agoniston (Greek – National Organisation of Cypriot Fighters)
FCO	Foreign and Commonwealth Office
GBE	Knight Grand Cross of the Order of the British Empire
Gen	General
GHQ	General Headquarters
GOC	General Officer Commanding
GPD	General Police Duties
GPMG	General Purpose Machine Gun
HK	Heckler & Koch
HMA	Her Majesty's Ambassador
HQNI	Headquarters Northern Ireland
HRT	High Readiness Team
IED	Improvised Explosive Device
IC	in charge
Inf	Infantry
IRA	Irish Republican Army
ISAF	International Security Assistance Force
JNCO	Junior Non Commissioned Officer
KCB	Knight Commander of the Bath
KFOR	Kosovo Force (NATO)
KMS	Kini Mini Services
LCpl	Lance Corporal
LMG	Light Machine Gun
LRA	Lords Rebel Army
Lt	Lieutenant
Lt Col	Lieutenant Colonel
Lt Gen	Lieutenant General
LZ	Landing Zone
Maj	Major
Maj Gen	Major General
MBE	Member of the Most Excellent Order of the British Empire
MC	Military Cross
MCP	Malayan Communist Party
ME	Middle East
MELF	Middle East Land Forces
MFP	Military Foot Police

Mk	Mark (as in 'Mark IV')
MNLA	Malayan National Liberation Army
MPAJA	Malayan People's Anti-Japanese Army
MSM	Meritorious Service Medal
MT	Motor Transport
NATO	North Atlantic Treaty Organisation
NAAFI	Navy, Army, Airforce Institute
NICRA	Northern Ireland Civil Rights Association
NCO	Non-Commissioned Officer
OC	Officer Commanding
OBE	Officer of the Most Excellent Order of the British Empire
OP	Operation
Para	Parachute
PDT	Pre-deployment training
PES	Personal Escort Section
PJHQ	Permanent Joint Headquarters
Pl	Platoon
PM(A)	Provost Marshal (Army)
Pro	Provost
Pte	Private
QGM	Queen's Gallantry Medal
QRF	Quick Reaction Force
RAO	Regimental Administrative Officer
RAFP	Royal Air Force Police
RCT	Royal Corps of Transport
RDT	Rapid Deployment Team
REME	Royal Electrical Mechanical Engineers
RM	Royal Marines
RMP	Royal Military Police
RMPTC	Royal Military Police Training Centre
RPG	Rocket Propelled Grenade
RSM	Regimental Sergeant Major
RTW	Regimental Training Wing
RUC	Royal Ulster Constabulary
SAP	Security Advance Party
SAS	Special Air Service
SACEUR	Supreme Allied Commander Europe

LIST OF ABBREVIATIONS

SEC	Spezial Einsatz Kommando
Sect	Section
Sgt	Sergeant
SHAPE	Supreme Headquarters Allied Powers Europe
SLR	Self Loading Rifle
SMG	Sub machine gun
SMPS	Special Mobile Provost Section
SSgt	Staff Sergeant
SIB	Special Investigation Branch
SOXMIS	Soviet Mission
Sqn	Squadron
TAOR	Tactical Area of Operation
UIN	Unit Identification Number
UN	United Nations
VE	Victory in Europe
VIP	Very Important Person
WAAC	Women's Army Auxiliary Corps
WO1	Warrant Officer Class 1
WO2	Warrant Officer 2
WRAC	Women's Royal Army Corps
WRAF	Women's Royal Air Force

A Principal's View

The Right Honourable
The Lord Ashdown of Norton-sub-Hamdon GCMG, KBE, PC

In turbulent times it's a comfort to know that there's a body of Her Majesty's Foot Police that is skilled and resourced to provide the best possible close protection. I have been privileged to experience the work of the Royal Military Police Close Protection Unit, first hand, as a frequent 'user' of their provision. Serving as the High Representative for Bosnia between 2002-2006, I encountered the RMP at very close quarters and found their expertise and professionalism to be second to none. Dealing with the likes of Karadzic, Izetbegovic and Milosovic, it was reassuring to know that I was always supported by my discreet, yet potentially lethal, CP team.

RMP Close Protection has a long and illustrious history. Originated in the embers of a defeated Nazi Germany, the Close Protection Unit has played a role in just about every post war British military occurrence or intervention; Northern Ireland, the Falklands, Iraq and Afghanistan. All these and more have seen the men and women of CPU perform bravely in the most trying of

From Left: Lt Gen William E 'Kip' Ward, Comd Stabilization Force, Sgt Shephard RMP, Lord Ashdown, Bill Clinton.

circumstances. Drawing from this illustrious heritage and ever resourceful and adaptable, I am confident that the 'Principals' of today will continue to receive first class protection.

Richard Keightley's authorised history is as timely as it is compelling and engaging. It takes the reader through the development of the Close Protection Branch and the doctrine that underpinned its ways of working. In reviewing recent training and operations, he has demonstrated the remarkable versatility of Close Protection and its transition from Branch to today's 'Unit'. I have to say that there is no better authority here than Richard; his own career has seen him in Burundi, Uganda and Sudan in support of the Foreign and Commonwealth Office, as well as a tour in Afghanistan as Team Leader for the NATO Ambassador. That he has found time to write this history whilst busy on operations is impressive alone! Suffice to say, this work is long overdue and it is one I warmly commend to you.

Vane Cottage
September 2014

Foreword

General Sir Nick Parker KCB CBE
Former Commander Land Forces

I have benefited from RMP Close Protection in 4 very different operational theatres over the past 10 years. Each time they have been highly professional, discrete and prepared to meet any eventuality. CP Teams allow commanders to concentrate on the things that matter. They are a significant enabler and one that we will need for many years to come in the complex security environments we will face. This history is an important record of many years of dedicated service.

Preface

The concept of Close Protection within the British Army is not a novel one and accounts of high ranking officials and military commanders being protected by an individual or an entire regiment are not new with examples found as far back as the Second Anglo-Boer War, where General Buller's Military Mounted Police orderly also acted as his de facto bodyguard with this practice continuing throughout World War I. It was during the interwar years that the British Military Police was first called upon to protect civilian VIPs also referred to as the 'Principal'.

Although the Military Police have always had a responsibility, albeit as Military Mounted Police, Military Foot Police, Corps of Military Police and, latterly, Royal Military Police for escorting senior commanders in operational theatres, and Her Majesty's Ambassadors and High Commissioners in high risk appointments abroad, it was not until the nineteen eighties that the Royal Military Police (RMP) officially became the lead authority on Close Protection within the British Armed forces. Members of the RMP, Royal Marine Police Troop and Royal Air Force Police are now deployed all around the world protecting VIPs from harm, be it the drug cartels in South America, Al Qaeda in Africa or the Taliban in Afghanistan. Whether the threat against a VIP is posed by a terrorist or criminal, the level of protection provided by the Military Police remains one of professionalism, dedication and unquestionable loyalty towards the Principal. In the pages that follow I have tried to encompass as much as possible about Close Protection (CP) and VIP escorts conducted by the RMP, from both my own experiences and from drawing upon the accounts of others. I have included a small insight into the campaigns that have led to the requirement for CP, in order to give a fuller picture of the environment together with the odd footnote to fill in the gaps. It is hoped that those who have contributed or who were involved at the time can reflect upon how they helped to lay the foundations of RMP CP as we know it today and that those who are new to the Corps, or are just interested, can see where it all began in order, perhaps, to decide where it is going. Before you press on and, for no other reason than it is a moment in history in which we (the RMP) had a small part to play that I could not include later on, I must mention

Capt Gerald Joseph Mullan, who was appointed as Personal Bodyguard to the Prime Minister Harold Macmillan during his historic visit to Moscow in February 1959. By no means is this work a complete account, but hopefully you will enjoy it.

Acknowledgements

This project started a number of years ago with the expectation it would be a few pages long. As time went on, I was astonished at the level of interest and willingness by those listed below, which led to the production of this book. To them all I owe my sincerest thanks and gratitude. Without their help, it would have remained a couple of pages long with a few dodgy photos of men with moustaches.

Gen Sir Nick Parker KCB CBE, former Commander Land Forces
Mr Mark Sedwill, former NATO Ambassador Afghanistan
Brig E O 'Eddy' Forster-Knight OBE
Sir Sherard Cowper-Coles KCMG CMG LVO
Brig (Ret'd) Collin Findlay MBE RMP
Brig (Ret'd) Jack Thomas OBE RMP
Col Jeremy Green OBE Regt Secretary RMP
Col Ian Prosser OBE RMP
Col (Ret'd) JH Baber MBE
Lt Col IAR Stenning MBE RMP
Lt Col (Ret'd) Kevin Bacon RMP
Lt Col (Ret'd) Ken Blake BEM RMP
Lt Col (Ret'd) Mick Bottomley BEM RMP
Lt Col (Ret'd) Stuart McLean RMP
Lt Col (Ret'd) Colin Watkins FLS RMP
Lt Col (Ret'd) Patrick Wellington MBE RMP
Maj Martin Pickford RMP
Maj (Ret'd) Allan Barley RMP
Maj (Ret'd) Julian Backler RMP
Maj (Ret'd) Bob Evans RMP
Maj (Retd) Ken Greenland QPM RMP
Maj (Ret'd) Geoff Harland RMP SIB
Maj (Ret'd) Charlie Millar RMP
Capt Lucy Close RMP
Capt Kirk Davies RMP

Capt Jim Devenney RMP
Capt 'Taff' Pike RMP
Capt Jim Shea RMP
Capt (Ret'd) Paul Allan RMP
Capt (Ret'd) Robert Eggelton RMP (V)
Capt (Ret'd) Derek Hall RMP
Capt (Ret'd) Colin Whatman RMP
WO1 (RSM) Neil Ashton RMP
WO1 (RSM) Mark Ingram RMP
Ex WO1 (RSM) Bernard Hudson RMP
Ex WO1 (RSM) Tony Johnson RMP
Ex WO1 (RSM) Eddie Monks RMP
Ex WO1 (RSM) John O'Donnell BEM RMP
Ex WO1 (RSM) Royton Oswick RMP
Ex WO1 (RSM) 'Percy' Powell RMP
Ex WO1 (RSM) Brian Samways RMP SIB
Ex WO1 (RSM) 'Wurze' Young RMP
Ex WO2 Danny Mander CMP
Ex WO2 Andy Mudd RMP
Ex WO2 Paul 'Shep' Shephard RMP
Ex WO2 Paul Tyrer RMP
WO2 Andy Gibson RMP
Ex WO2 Colin Carnall RMP
Ex WO2 Dave Duxbury RMP
Ex WO2 Ian Hollas RMP
Ex WO2 Brian Lumley RMP
SSgt Harry Dearing RMP
SSgt Micky McLean RMP
Ex SSgt Geoff Berry RMP
Ex SSgt Neil Cowen RMP
Ex SSgt Denzil Cowley RMP
Ex SSgt 'Flash' Hannan RMP
Ex SSgt John 'Perry' Mason RMP
Ex SSgt Andy McMath RMP
Ex SSgt John Redman RMP
Ex SSgt William Sheridan BEM
Ex SSgt Frederick 'Woody' Woodward RMP

Sgt Ben Bosworth RMP
Sgt Paul Burton RMP
Sgt Andy Heron RMP
Ex Sgt Bob Adams RMP SIB
Ex Sgt Andy Cooper RMP
Ex Sgt Mick Dale RMP
Ex Sgt 'Punchy' Pete Glover RMP
Ex Sgt Stewart Leach RMP
Ex Sgt Ray Spence RMP
Cpl Mick Collier RMP
Cpl Steve Grey RMP
Cpl Steve 'Longlegs' Rowbottom RMP
Ex Cpl Mike Aldworth RMP
Ex Cpl Tony Bowlder RMP
Ex Cpl Drew Bowness RMP
Ex Cpl Polly Cairns RMP
Ex Cpl Steve Carr RMP
Ex Cpl Peter Clinch RMP
Ex Cpl Stuart Graham RMP
Ex Cpl Derrick Griffin RMP
Ex Cpl Ian Hay RMP
Ex Cpl Dennis Jobling RMP
Ex Cpl Ben Slater RMP
Ex Cpl Norman Walter RMP
Ex LCpl Douglas Austen RMP
Ex LCpl Gordon Chick RMP
Ex LCpl David S Davies RMP
Ex LCpl Mike Foster RMP
Ex LCpl Malcolm Keates RMP
Ex LCpl Alan Marsh RMP
Ex LCpl Mick Parry RMP
Keith Wiseman, The Royal British Legion
Richard Callaghan, RMP Corps Museum
Ruth Kusionowicz, *Soldier Magazine*
Roy Elvis, Champ Spares UK Ltd
Janet Martinez, MM Publishing United States
Wendy McMullen, CPU

Nigel Chapman, Nigel Chapman Photography

Allyson Gray, formally CPU

Peter Elliot, Dept of Research and Information Services, Royal Air Force Museum

Calum Laird & Bull McLoughlin, Commando © D.C.Thomson & Co Ltd

Headquarters Recruiting Group Army Recruiting Team

NATO DEFINITION OF CLOSE PROTECTION

The preventative and reactive measures taken by trained personnel to protect a person, who is specifically or generally at threat from assassination, kidnapping or other illegal act.

Chapter 1

The Early Years

Although Close Protection within the RMP as we understand it today heralded from the early days of the troubles in Northern Ireland, RMP Close Protection in the modern world can find its roots embedded in the history of World Wars I and II. WO1 Francis Lloyd Willis, (pictured overleaf with The Prince of Wales, and future King Edward VIII), who had transferred into the Military Mounted Police from the 1st Royal Dragoons in 1915, was appointed as the personal dispatch rider to King George V. The trend continued and in World War Two a dare-devil motorcyclist, Cpl Ronald Pope CMP[1] became the personal outrider to Lt General (later General) Sir Miles Dempsey GBE, KCB, DSO, MC[2] and saw service in Italy, Sicily, France and Belgium. Ronald also escorted the British Prime Minister Winston Churchill to the front line. Following the Japanese attack on Pearl Harbor in 1941, China offered support to the Allies by providing vital logistical assistance throughout the Burma campaign. It was because of this interaction between China and the allied powers that the Chinese nationalist leader, Generalissimo Chiang Kai-shek and his wife were given a CMP escort in November 1943 whilst attending the Cairo Conference[3] in Egypt.

Also in Cairo as a member of 201 Provost Company was LCpl Charles Poulson CMP who recounted in the RMP Journal of April 1999 the following:

> Then came a spell at the British Embassy guarding Lord Killairn's children

---

1   The Military Mounted Police (MMP) and Military Foot Police (MFP) were merged in 1926 to form the Corps of Military Police (CMP). In 1946 the Corps was awarded the 'Royal' prefix in recognition of the service given by the Corps during World War Two.
2   General Sir Miles Christopher Dempsey, GBE, KCB, DSO, MC (15 December 1896 – 5 June 1969) survived two and a half years of bitter fighting as an infantry officer on the Western Front before accompanying his beloved Royal Berkshire Regiment in the little-known North West Persia campaign of 1920-21. In six years, he rose from Major to command over half a million men in the largest combined operation in history, leading them to victory a year later. He was later commander of the British Second Army during the D-Day landings in World War II.
3   The Cairo Conference (codenamed Sextant) was held between 22-26 November 1943 at the residence of the U.S. Ambassador to Egypt, Alexander Kirk. The conference was attended by U.S. President Franklin Roosevelt, British Prime Minister Winston Churchill and China's Generalissimo Chiang Kai-shek. The agenda of the conference was to discuss the allied position against Japan during the war and what direction was to be taken in post war Asia.

WO1 Francis Lloyd Willis with The Prince of Wales, and future King Edward VIII.

CMP Escort to Generalissimo and Madame Chiang Kai-shek in Cairo 1943.

as they played on the Embassy lawn; their lives had been threatened by a terrorist group, the Stern Gang. The Embassy stood on the banks of the Nile and part of my duty was to keep all boats beyond a marked boundary on the river with instructions to machine gun any that came too near. The Yalta Middle East Conference was another memorable occasion. Groups of us were detailed to bodyguard Churchill, Roosevelt, Stalin and King Ibn Saud of Arabia. The main guard consisted of two rings of troops of some hundred heavily armed men surrounding the buildings and special service men inside. I was one of eight assigned to escort and guard Winston Churchill. At the end of the conference, each group of guards was paraded to receive the formal thanks of the dignitaries. The King was the first to show his appreciation and he presented each of his guards with a watch. Interest in the 'formal' thanks then intensified but those looking after Churchill were to be disappointed – he asked for our pocket books and returned them with his signature!

The relationship between the Military Police and Winston Churchill continued when Cpl (later WO2) Danny Mander CMP was appointed as Churchill's bodyguard during the Tehran Conference[4] in 1943.

In 1944 a section of CMP from HQ 21st Army Group Provost Coy commanded by Lt Mills CMP escorted General Bernard Montgomery as 21st Army Group and the US 12 Army Group moved to Normandy remaining with him for the duration of the campaign. In October of that year, King George VI was visiting the British 2nd Army in Belgium and together with Lt General Dempsey was provided with an escort from the CMP. Lt General Dempsey later became the first Colonel Commandant of the Royal Military Police but it was during the visit to Belgium that he was knighted by the King, the last 'warrior' to be knighted by a monarch on the field of battle. Winston Churchill was again provided with an escort during his visit to the ruins of Berlin on the first day of the Potsdam Conference[5] on 16th July 1945. Following VE day, in the British Zone of West Germany, Headquarters British

---

4   The Tehran Conference was a meeting between Joseph Stalin, Franklin D. Roosevelt and Winston Churchill between 28 November and December 1, 1943, held at the Soviet Embassy in Tehran, Iran. The aim of the conference was to plan the final strategy for the war against Nazi Germany and its allies; the chief discussion was centered on the opening of a second front in Western Europe.
5   The Potsdam Conference was held at Cecilienhof in Potsdam, occupied Germany between 16th July and 2nd August 1945. Delegates were the British Prime Minister Sir Winston Churchill, U.S. President Harry Truman and Soviet Union Communist Party General Secretary Joseph Stalin. The purpose of the conference was to decide how to administer post-war Nazi Germany, who had unconditionally surrendered nine weeks earlier.

Prime Minister Winston Churchill visits the ruins of Berlin whilst attending the Postdam Conference in July 1945. The escort provided by members of the CMP.

Army on the Rhine, (HQ BAOR), became responsible for the protection of British VIPs and VVIPs visiting BAOR units and the Commander- in-Chief's Committee was responsible for ordering the various levels of protection for the visitors, dependent upon the prevailing threat. The responsibility for providing the armed escorts fell upon Provost Marshal BAOR and the Corp of Military Police (CMP) were set to task and afforded protection to British Royalty, the Prime Minister and Cabinet Members and Military Commanders. Montgomery, himself, was afforded Military Police protection when visiting British Troops in Austria (BTA) whilst appointed as Chief of the Imperial General Staff c1946. Again, in c1949, he was afforded protection when a detachment of Military Policemen was provided from 105 Pro Coy RMP, then commanded by Maj George Pilitz.

Escort duties were often random and would fall upon a responsible Officer or NCO available at the time. Major (later Lieutenant Colonel) Harold Dibbens SIB was serving under Lt Col Rupert L. Warburton DPM Palestine and Transjordan, Syria and Lebanon, when he was appointed as bodyguard to

Corporal Ronald Pope CMP and unknown colleague as outrider to the VIP escort section.

Field Marshal Viscount Montgomery of Alamein with his RMP
Escort Section whilst visiting troops in Austria c1946

Viscount Montgomery of Alamein's escort provided by members of 105 Pro Coy RMP during his visit to Austria c1946.

HRH The Duke of Gloucester for three days whilst the Duke visited military hospitals, the Palace at Amman, the Polish Brigade and other units within Jerusalem and the command.

In 1945, Montgomery was visiting 43 Div in Celle, Germany, to review troops with Maj Gen Thomas GOC 43 Div. Throughout his visit, Monty was escorted by Lance Corporal (later Sergeant) George Whiting CMP 43 Div Pro Coy. (George took a photograph during the visit that was signed by the Field Marshal through a strange quirk of fate some years later and can be seen over).

Later, in 1951, LCpl Geoff Berry RMP was a part of Paris Echelon Provost Section based in Fontainbleau, at the time, home of the Supreme Headquarters Allied Power Europe (SHAPE) with Field Marshal Montgomery as Deputy Supreme Commander to Gen Dwight Eisenhower. Montgomery's residence was the Chateau Courances and a Protection Section was permanently detached there. Although LCpl Berry was assigned as security to SHAPE, he joined the section at the Chateau on a number of occasions and, together with them, escorted the Field Marshal on his local travels.

As the years passed, the CMP, and later RMP, were called upon to offer protection within different theatres of operation and countries being visited by VVIPs including the British Foreign Secretary, Anthony Eden during his visit

28 DETER SUPPRESS EXTRACT!

Photograph taken by Sgt George Whiting CMP of Field Marshal Montgomery visiting Celle, 1945 (Inset – Sgt George Whiting)

The Escort Section appointed to the British Foreign Minister, Anthony Eden setting off from the HQ British Military Government in the Olympic Stadium during his visit to the British Commander-in-Chief Mission Soviet Forces in Germany (BRIXMIS) Berlin, 1953.

to the British Sector in Berlin in 1953. The crowning glory, however, was back in 1952 when the RMP can take credit for being the first 'Close Protection Team' afforded to the current monarch, Queen Elizabeth II.

At the invite of Major Eric Sherbrooke Walker MC and his wife Lady 'Bettie', Princess Elizabeth and her husband the Duke of Edinburgh, visited Kenya in February 1952. It was when staying overnight at the Walker's Treetops Lodge in Aberdare National Park whilst on safari that news reached the group that King George VI had died peacefully in his sleep at Sandringham. Through Royal Ascension the princess had become Queen and, as a result, the new Queen of England was afforded an armed escort provided by Sgt RW (Dickie) Fettes, Cpl Jack Craddock and LCpls Elston, Morton, Heath and Burford, all members of 618 Special Mobile Provost Section (SMPS), RMP East Africa Command, who ensured both Her Majesty and the Duke of Edinburgh arrived safely at Nanyuki Airport before their onward journey back to the United Kingdom.

This was not the only escort duty that 618 SMPS performed in East Africa. During the Mau Mau Uprising[6], the section were escorting General Sir George Erskine GCB, KBE, DSO, GOC in Chief East Africa Command, (pictured right), on patrol in the Aberdare National Park, about 100 miles from Nairobi. The only vehicle to be making progress through the dense undergrowth of bamboo was a 'Caterpillar' bulldozer and, not to be deterred, the General climbed aboard. To his right was his bodyguard, Cpl Derrick Griffin RMP with Cpl Harry Lacey RMP walking alongside. During his time in Kenya, Cpl Griffin, together with other members of the unit, spent much of their time escorting the General and other dignitaries.

The photograph on page 31 featured in an article in the December 1953 issue of *Soldier Magazine,* headlined, "They Attack from the Jeep heads".

LCpl Griffin continued to work with the General during his tour of Kenya and recalls the opportunities that Close Protection afforded even in the fifties. Flying from a dusty airstrip, the General visited Merus, in central Kenya. Formerly known as the Eastern Province, Merus was a small town and District Headquarters sited on the slopes of Mount Kenya. The General stayed at the

---

6　The Mau Mau Uprising was a military conflict that took place in Kenya (then called British East Africa), from 1952 to 1960, between a Kikuyu-dominated, anti-colonial group called Mau Mau and the British Army. The conflict set the stage for Kenyan independence and motivated Africans in other colonies to fight against colonialism. It created a rift between the European colonial community in Kenya and the Home Office in London, but also resulted in violent divisions within the Kikuyu community.

General Sir George Erskine GCB, KBE, DSO, GOC in Chief East Africa Command.

Photograph showing members of 618 Special Mobile Provost Section RMP, East Africa Command, the first military escort to H.M. The Queen taken at Nyeri Airstrip in February 1952. The NCOs are Sgt RW (Dickie) Fettes, Cpl Jack Craddock and LCpls Heath, Burford, Elston and Morton. This article featured in the *RMP Corps Journal*.

THE EARLY YEARS

As featured in *Soldier Magazine*, "They Attack from the Jeep heads".

'Pig & Whistle' lodge, on the Nkubu Road. Tasked by Sgt Fettes to escort the General on the plane, the rest of the section were to catch up the following day. Arriving at the lodge, Cpl Griffin visited the dining room for dinner. General Erskine was already seated in the corner so, as is the way in such circles, Cpl Griffin kept himself discreet sitting at another table with a sergeant from the REME. Soon afterwards, the General's aide approached the table and invited Cpl Griffin to join the General for dinner. Naturally LCpl Griffin could hardly refuse and recalls that it was a surreal moment; an 18 year old lad from Walsall sharing the dinner table with a General and Knight of the Realm. The evening passed very pleasantly and LCpl Griffin credits that evening with the General as the one that changed his outlook on life and helped shape his future. This is one of many examples of how the bodyguard enters into a completely different relationship with senior military commanders and senior civilian officials from that of anyone within that circle.

Following the withdrawal of Japan from Malaya at the end of World War II, the Malayan economy was left in a state of disruption. Problems included unemployment, low wages, and scarce and expensive food. There was considerable labour unrest and a large number of strikes occurred between 1946 and 1948. The British administration was attempting to repair Malaya's

The De Havilland DH 89 Dragon Rapide, a Kenyan charter plane on which LCpl Griffin escorted General Erskine.

From Left: Army Press Officer (name unknown), Captain Fennick-Clennel ADC to General Erskine, pictured centre, extreme right, Brigadier Lord Thurlo, all enjoying a cup of tea with LCpl Wood and Cpl Len Warne of the Escort Section in the background. Note the General's revolver attached to his Sam Browne.

economy quickly, especially as revenue from Malaya's tin and rubber industries was important to Britain's own post-war recovery. As a result, protesters were dealt with harshly, by measures including arrest and deportation. In turn, protesters became increasingly militant and on 16 June 1948, the first overt act of the war[7] took place when three European plantation managers were killed at Sungai Siput, Perak.

The Colonial administration brought emergency measures into law, first in Perak, in response to the Sungai Siput incident and then, in July, country-wide. Under the measures, the Malayan Communist Party (MCP) and other leftist parties were outlawed and the police were given the power to imprison communists and intern those suspected of assisting them. The MCP, led by Chin Peng, retreated to rural areas, and formed the Malayan National Liberation Army (MNLA). The MNLA began a guerrilla campaign, targeting mainly the colonial resource industries of tin mining and rubber plantations.

The MNLA was partly a re-formation of the Malayan People's Anti-Japanese Army (MPAJA), the MCP-led guerrilla force, which had been the principal resistance in Malaya against the Japanese occupation, and who had been secretly trained and armed by the British during the later stages of World War II. Disbanded in December 1945, the MPAJA officially surrendered its weapons to the Military. However, many weapons were not returned and it was with these weapons that the MNLA commonly employed guerrilla tactics to sabotage installations, attack rubber plantations or destroy transportation and infrastructure. This campaign lasted until 1960. Victory came to the commonwealth security forces against the communist 'terrorists'.

It was during this time, between 1952 and 1953, that Cpl Bill Hill RMP, a national serviceman, was posted with 40 Infantry Division Provost at Kluang Garrison, where he was assigned 'special duties', which, in turn, saw him appointed as the personal bodyguard to the Brigade Commander (Bde Comd) Brigadier Charlie Howard. Given the level of the threat by the terrorists, he was 'armed to the teeth' and given a Vauxhall Vanguard staff car with driver to transport the Brigadier. A regular visitor was the C-in-C Far East Land Forces, General Sir Charles Keightley[8], who travelled with Brigadier Howard

---

7   The MNLA termed the conflict as the *Anti-British National Liberation War*. However, the rubber plantations and tin mining industries had pushed for the use of the term "emergency" since their losses would not have been covered by Lloyd's insurers if it had been termed a 'war'. Subsequently, the 'war' was referred to as 'The Malayan Emergency' by the colonial government.
8   General Sir Charles Frederic Keightley, GCB, GBE, DSO (24 June 1901 – 17 June 1974) was a senior officer in the British Army during and following World War II. In August 1951, he became

A Humber Snipe similar to the one used by the C-in-C.

on a regular basis. Often, both the Bde Comd and C-in-C would travel by helicopter to visit troops on the ground and Cpl Hill and his driver would race by road in the Vauxhall in an attempt to keep up with the officers in the air so they could be driven around the area after they landed. On one such occasion, Cpl Hill was invited to join the VIP party in the helicopter and when it landed the Aide-de-Camp to the General produced a picnic hamper and was instructed by the General to supply Cpl Hill with lunch, which he did, with a couple of sandwiches and a bottle of 'Tiger' beer. During these travels, the Brigadier had discovered that Cpl Hill was a keen cricketer and, one afternoon, he phoned the Brigade Headquarters requesting that he be released to play cricket in Seremban against the Brigade Headquarters in the Sembilan area. Cpl Hill's sergeant called him a 'jammy sod' and the place on the team was assured. The next problem was the issue of cricket whites, not in abundance in the middle of a conflict. The Brigadier, having a fatherly manner about him, stepped in and loaned Cpl Hill his own flannels. After a two-day match with a few runs under his belt, Cpl Hill returned to Kluang and, after cleaning and pressing the whites, returned them to the Brigadier.

LCpl Gordon Chick was serving with 17 Gurkha Infantry Div Pro Coy RMP in Johor Bahru, Malaya in 1956 when he and another LCpl provided an armed motorcycle escort to the British Advisor (BA), Johor State. Within the Town Board Limits, they would be dressed in shorts and full whites, which though not safe by any of today's standards, seemed practical in Malaya. On one occasion, however, the pair were engulfed in very heavy rain, which, when combined with riding a motorcycle, made a real mess of the uniform. When dropping the BA off at his residence he remarked how sorry he was that the

---

the Commander-in-Chief, Far East Land Forces with the rank of general. Between 1953 and 1957, he was Commander-in-Chief Middle East Land Forces, which included the period of the Suez Crisis. Keightley was C-in-C of Operation Musketeer, an Anglo-French-Israeli plan for the invasion of Egypt to capture the Suez Canal during the Suez Crisis. Israel had the additional objective to open the Straits of Tiran. Incidentally, the General is no relation to the author.

NCOs ended up in such a state. LCpl Chick continued escort duties and on 27th September 1957 both he and Cpl Narsing drove to RAF Butterworth to meet up with General Sir Charles Keightley, to escort him to a Pass Out Parade at the Brigade of Gurkhas Far East Training Depot in Sungani Patani, a distance of approximately 90 kilometers. The C-in-C was being driven in a Humber Super Snipe staff car (pictured over) with the ADC in front with the driver with LCpl Chick leading in a Mk1 Land Rover. The C-in-C was keen to make the most of his staff car and all LCpl Chick saw in his rear-view mirror was the ADC waving for him to drive faster. With his foot to the floor both vehicles 'shot through' police checkpoints to make the parade in good time. The C-in-C was then escorted back to RAF Butterworth and a waiting Dakota airplane. Cpl Narsing and LCpl Chick then spent the night at Ipoh Detachment before setting off on the 455km journey back to HQ in Seremban.

In 1953, members of 512 SMPS Royal Military Police and 203 Provost Company Royal Military Police supported the Suez Campaign. 22503279 LCpl Bryan Waller RMP was one of the JNCOs to deploy on a very turbulent 18 month tour of the region but it wasn't until the last six months of the campaign that his proudest moment came when he and LCpl Mick Wells RMP were given a Willys jeep and appointed personal escort to the Brigade Commander.

After being commissioned into the Royal Artillery in May 1947, Capt Derek Hall transferred to Provost Duties on 1 December 1950, before being posted to the newly formed 6th Armoured Division Provost Company in Bulford in February the following year. The Division moved to Germany in February, 1952, and Capt Hall was appointed as the Motor Transport Officer (MTO). One of his tasks was to take two drivers to 193 (Ports) Coy RMP in Hamburg, where they collected two Jeeps that had been equipped for escort duties. The vehicles had been fitted with large American sirens and a red flashing light on the off-side wing. The sirens were quickly changed to four tone martin horns and the red lights to blue.

That was to be Capt Hall's first exposure to VIP escorts and in 1953 he saw a posting to 101 (HQ BAOR) Provost Company in Bad Oeynhausen, Germany, where he became a member of the VIP Escort Section and was responsible for the safety of the Rt Hon Anthony Eden, then Foreign Secretary. Until 15th May 1955, the British Army was still an occupying force so all escorts were armed with a round-chambered. During his time with the RMP, Capt Hall also escorted General Westmorland, US Commander SHAPE and

HRH Princess Margaret's RMP escort section during her visit to Germany in 1954.

Field Marshal Montgomery, who had assumed the appointment of Deputy Commander. Capt Hall, with LCpl M Byard driving, also had occasion to provide protection for HRH the Duke of Edinburgh on 18 March 1953 (after a meeting in the middle of the ranges the Duke was taken for a ride in a tank by General Sir GE Prior-Palmer), the Duke of Gloucester (a Major General in his own right and Colonel-in-Chief Royal Army Service Corps (RASC)[9]), and even the Russian Commander-in-Chief on his visit to the SOXMIS mission at Bad Salzuflen, who was being hosted by General Sir Richard Gale.

In May 1954, HRH Princess Margaret visited Germany for engagements with various VIPs and dignitaries including the West German President Konrad Adenauer. 2 Div Pro Coy were given the task of protecting the Princess and Capt Hall was once again called upon and led an armed escort, which included two Series 1 Land Rovers, a German police Opel at the rear and an American Jeep taking the lead, in which was Cpl Mike Aldworth RMP, Maj Davis RMP with LCpl Gordon Officer RMP driving (pictured over). The Princess was met at Wahn Airfield on a very damp day and was to be escorted to Bonn to meet the East German Chancellor. Princess Margaret was being driven in her own Rolls Royce with the escort vehicles at the front and rear travelling about 50mph, which was quite fast enough on wet cobbles in primitive, four-wheel-drive vehicles. Princess Margaret, however, had other ideas. Following some flashing of Rolls Royce headlights, the convoy came to a halt and the aide left the Rolls Royce, approached and explained to Maj Davies that the Princess suggested the convoy should travel a little quicker. Subsequently, the aide returned to the Rolls Royce and all vehicles overtook the stationary Jeep at

---

9   RASC Royal Army Service Corps, which later became the Royal Logistic Corps (RLC).

a speed far more suited to a Princess. The Jeep dropped in behind the German police car at the rear and the driver, although doing his very best to keep up, lost control of the vehicle on the wet cobbles and spun off the road, down a bank and into a field. There were no injuries and after finding the exit to the field the companions rejoined the road. However, the VIP convoy was nowhere to be seen. Finally, the three arrived at Bonn with Cpl Aldworth commenting that their faces matched the colour of their caps. At this stage, still no formal escort training had been received and issued revolvers and ammunition were still kept separately from each other.

This incident led to a conversation between Capt Hall and the Provost Marshal regarding the use of suitable vehicles when operating in the escort role. Ultimately, the complaint was taken to the CinC and new vehicles in the form of four white Opel Kapitans with folding roofs and radio telephones and a VW Van with a radio base station installed arrived at 101 Pro Coy in short order.

Capt Hall's adventures did not stop there and, in 1955, he had the opportunity to drive the Archbishop of Canterbury to Church House in Iserlohn in the C-in-C's Rolls Royce in order for him to address all the Padres in the Command. On the 25th July of the same year back home in the UK, whilst serving with 158 Company in Aldershot, Corporal Dudley Allum joined a section under the command of Sgt Freddie Ford, which was tasked with providing armed security to the Bicentenary Review of the Kings Royal Rifle Corps by Her Majesty the Queen. Being a proven shot with a revolver, Cpl Allum was a sensible choice for the task and, wearing full duty order with 'whites', carrying a loaded revolver, he provided the security on the wings. In today's security arena, this would be one of the layers of the 'security onion' and as important as those officers appointed to protect the VIP directly. With a suspected break-in at the armoury at Aborfield with the loss of some weapons and increased activity by the IRA reported, every armed officer had his part to play. Thankfully, the day passed without incident and Corporal Allum returned to Aldershot.

1956 saw a week-long visit to Monchengladbach, Germany, by HRH the Princess Royal (Princess Mary), the Queen's Aunt, in her role as Colonel-in-Chief of the Corps of Royal Signals and Capt Hall provided the escort for the visit. Whilst on a short journey on a Sunday morning from the Commander-in-Chief's house to church, a German police car was providing traffic control, when a motorcyclist failed to see the car and crashed his motorbike and side car. Capt Hall ordered the VIP vehicle to keep going and the second vehicle

Opel Kapitans with Escort Section ready and waiting outside 101 Pro Coy RMP circa 1955.

stopped to administer first aid. Later it was established that the young man had discharged himself from hospital but his passenger, a lady of the night, had remained in hospital with a fractured skull. The Princess was upset to hear the news and offered to send some fruit to her. Capt Hall convinced HRH that that probably was not quite the right thing to do and that he would speak with the German Chief of Police to ensure no prosecution would be made against the couple. Whether or not that was the case we shall never know.

In October 1951, following the overthrow of King Farouk of Egypt by General Neguib and Colonel Abd al-Nasser, the Egyptian Government abrogated the 1936 Anglo-Egyptian Treaty, which agreed to the British retaining a Military base in the Suez Canal Zone until mid-1956. As Britain still had about £100m worth of equipment stored in the Zone from the end of the war, and nearly 10,000 troops to oversee the protection and maintenance of the equipment, the British Government refused to accept the abrogation. Anti-British sentiment had accompanied the coup d'état with the Egyptian Government ordering its troops and police to harass British troops in the Zone. Very quickly this harassment escalated and many civilians with members of the Fedayeen were taking part. A 'Suez Emergency' was declared by Britain and an extra 6,000 men, 170 tons of stores and 330 vehicles were air-dispatched to the Zone in a matter of ten days, the swiftest build-up ever achieved by the British Army in peacetime.

The conventional threat eased but terrorist attacks against British military establishments in the Canal Zone increased, while the Egyptian Police refused to cooperate in maintaining security. Events came to a head during resistance to a 2 and 3 PARA cordon and search operation in Ismailia the same month, during which four terrorists were killed and 12 captured for the loss of one

THE EARLY YEARS 39

officer. The 1st Lancashire Fusiliers, meanwhile, fought a bloody battle to occupy a police barracks, supported by a Centurion tank, resulting in the killing or wounding of 95 policemen at a cost of four dead and 1 wounded.

At its peak this campaign involved about 80,000 Servicemen and women, made up of a large Army contingent, Royal Air Force Units, the Royal Marine Commandos and a Naval Squadron which constantly patrolled the Suez Canal. It was the largest Military Force to be engaged in any one military theatre since the end of World War Two. Not only was the campaign fought to protect British personnel and property in the Zone but it was also the time of the 'Cold War' and a Russian threat to the Middle East oilfields, which supplied Western Europe's oil, made the protection of the Canal supreme as it was considered vital to Britain's strategic interests, as it was Britain's lifeline to Australasia, the Far East and the African Colonies and was essential for trade between Europe and the Far East.

The emergency lasted between 16th October 1951 and 19th October 1954 and during this time about 600 servicemen died whilst on 'Active Service', due to actions of terrorists and ill-health brought on by the unhygienic conditions prevalent in the Canal Zone at that time. Because of the heightened threat, in 1951 Cpl DJ 'Shiner' Wright was posted to 203 Pro Coy at Moascar Garrison as Chief Clerk and, in 1952, he was promoted to Sergeant and appointed as the personal bodyguard and NCO ic Commander-in-Chief's Escort.

During 1954, Cpl (later WO1) Tony Johnson was serving in the Canal Zone and there were two dedicated special escort sections, 512 (commanded by 2Lt (later Brig) Brian Thomas CBE) and 615 SMPS, one based at GHQ Middle East Land Forces (MELF) in Fayid, its location before moving to Cyprus, and a second at HQ Canal Zone in Moascar. In addition, the GOC 1 and 3 Div also had a dedicated section appointed to them, which had at least two vehicles, a Jeep, Land Rover Mk1 or an Austin Champ[10], which could be armed with a grenade launcher and machine gun such as a Bren. The vehicles were not fitted with blue lights or sirens but did have a wire cutter mounted on the front bumper. In late 1954, whilst serving with 203 Pro Coy Egypt, LCpl Mick Parry RMP was part of the GOC 1 Div Escort Section and, when travelling by road, the GOC's driver would drive on one side of the road with the escort vehicles, one about 150 metres in front and one to the rear, on

---

10   The Austin Champ was designed by Alex Isigonis (Designer of the Austin Mini Car) at the end of WW2 to meet the requirements of the British Army for a fast attack combat vehicle to replace the American Jeep.

Bren Light Machine Gun .303 – Length: 1156mm – Weight: 11.25 kg (loaded) – Muzzle Velocity: 743.7m/s – Effective Range: 150m;

Jeep with mounted Bren gun.

the opposite side to prevent anyone from overtaking. In the same year, LCpl Malcolm Keates was posted to 1 Inf Div RMP and saw himself assigned to General Sir Charles Keightley, who was now C-in-C Far East Command, as part of his Escort Section along with SSgt Jim Alberson MM RMP and a section of JNCOs. The General lived in a house in Fayid on the shores of the Great Bitter Lake[11] about an hour from Cairo. During his time with the General, Cpl Keates remembers visits from Field Marshal Montgomery, Lady

---

11 The Great Bitter Lake is so named as it is composed of saltwater and serves as a waiting area for tankers and ships as they travel along the Suez Canal.

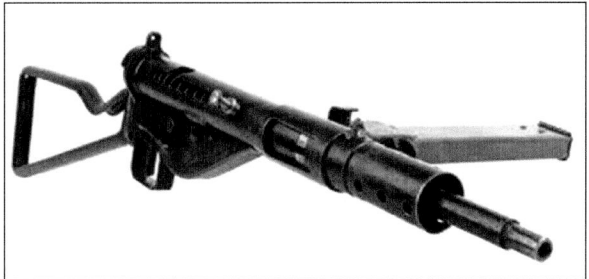

The 9mm Sten gun.

A Royal Military Police Austin Champ as used in Egypt.
Picture provided by Roy Elvis, Champ Spares UK Ltd.

Mountbatten and the actor Terry Thomas. Teresa 'Tessie' O'Shea[12], a Welsh actress and entertainer (and forces' favourite from World War II), also visited and Cpl Keates had the pleasure of collecting her from RAF Fayid. When they arrived back at the residence, Miss O'Shea ran up the steps to the General, who was waiting to receive her, and said "Hello darling", and promptly gave him a big kiss; not quite the method of introduction enjoyed by the General but no doubt one that was enjoyed nevertheless. During the visit by Montgomery,

---

12 Teresa "Tessie" O'Shea was an extremely popular entertainer who adopted "Two Ton Tessie from Tennessee" as her theme song owing to her larger- than- ideal size.

Escort Section in Al Imailiyah, Cpl Malcolm Keates can be seen driving the rear vehicle. Note the retrofitted wire cutter on the front of the lead vehicle, used to prevent decapitation by wire of the occupants that had been placed across the road for that purpose.

who was in Egypt to lecture to senior British and Egyptian officers from the Canal Zone, Cpl Keates was on duty around the residence and, whilst he was passing under the Field Marshal's bedroom, Montgomery came outside and greeted the Corporal, commenting on how nice the moon was reflecting on the lake and, after a short conversation, asking Cpl Keates if he wrote to his mother every week before retiring indoors!

Sadly, Cpl Keates did not enjoy many surreal moments such as that with Montgomery, and whilst he was driving between Fayid and Moascar about half an hour before the Field Marshal in an open top Canadian Ford car, Cpl Keates passed through a small village called Gebal Mayegm, near Ismailia, when he saw a person dressed in a white Galabea on a roof top. Cpl Keates also saw that the man had in his hands a Sten gun before hearing shots ring out. Cpl Keates was shot in the left knee and with blood flowing from the wound, he managed to keep the car moving and returned fire with his Smith & Wesson, hitting the assailant three times. Arriving at Malacar lift bridge, which was under the control of the Grenadier Guards, Keates reported the incident and the shooter was subsequently found and arrested, although no weapon was found. Thankfully, the bullet that had struck Cpl Keates had passed straight through causing minimal damage and he was back on duty in five weeks.

Meanwhile, trouble was brewing in Cyprus. The island had belonged to the Ottoman Empire and was annexed by the British during the First World War and, in 1925, it became a British Crown Colony. 'Enosis' (Greek-Cypriot union with Greece) was entirely unacceptable to Turkey, because of the strategic location of the island and she threatened it with annexation in 1954. When Greece rejected a power-sharing solution between herself, Britain and Turkey, Greek-Cypriots, who outnumbered their Turkish counterparts by four to one, took this to mean tacit Greek support for Union.

Ethniki Organosis Kyprion Agoniston (Greek for National Organisation of Cypriot Fighters) (EOKA) was a Greek Cypriot nationalist military resistance organisation, that fought for the end of British rule of Cyprus, as well as for self-determination and union with Greece. EOKA engaged to free the Greek Cypriots from British rule and the military campaign officially began at 0030hrs on 1st April, 1955. On this date, EOKA waged a pitiless campaign of terror against Cypriots to suppress even passive opposition . Selected muktars or village headmen and unarmed constables were murdered, frequently drenched in petrol and burned alive before their families. People were intimidated against speaking with the security forces and the reign of terror spread to include targets such as simultaneous attacks on the British controlled Cyprus Broadcasting Station in Nicosia, the British Army's Wolseley barracks, as well as Turkish civilians. Thereafter, and unlike other anti-colonial movements, EOKA confined its acts to sabotaging military installations, ambushing military convoys and patrols, and assassinating British soldiers and local informers. During the course of the insurrection, a total of 105 British servicemen were killed and 51 members of the local police force.

When MELF moved out of the Canal Zone, General Keightley, (and Cpl Keates), moved his HQ to Nicosia with his residence in Kyrenia about 15 miles north of Nicosia. The house was called 'The House on the Ridge' and overlooked the sea. The 'ridge' itself was extremely steep and afforded very good protection for the property due to the steep gradient. A high fence provided security in areas the ridge did not and an infantry platoon provided the outer perimeter patrols with one or two bodyguards being assigned to the house. The drive between the General's house and the HQ in Nicosia took a route through the mountains that with sheer drops on one side, trees and steep hills on the other coupled with hairpin bends made for a scary drive at the best of times but the environment was also ideal for the EOKA.

Webley Service Revolver 38: Length 266mm – Weight 1.1kg – Muzzle velocity 190m/s – Effective range 46m.

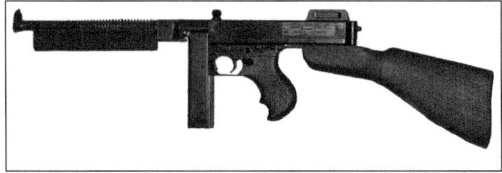

Thompson sub machine gun .45: Length 851mm – Weight 4.9kg – Muzzle velocity 280 m/s – Rate of fire 600-1200rpm – Effective range 50m.

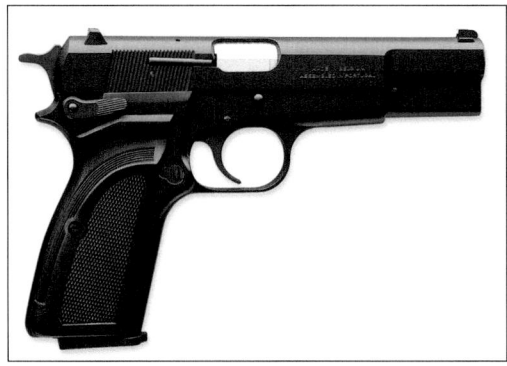

The Browning Hi Power pistol remained with RMP CP teams until 2001. Following a four week trial of the Sig Saur P226 pistol by then Cpl Keightley in 1996 at Longmoor, the RMP phased out the Browning as the primary personal weapon of the Close Protection Operator. The Sig Saur was introduced in 2001 with its successor, the P229 being adopted 2007.

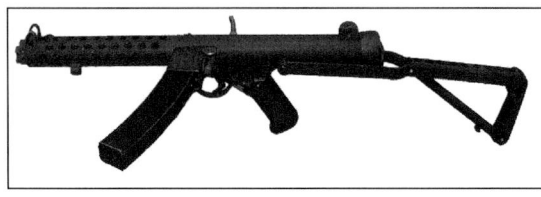

Sterling sub machine gun 9mm: Length 686mm – Weight 2.7kg – Rate of fire 550 rpm – Muzzle velocity 390 m/s – Effective range 200m.

Whilst the General was in the UK, some of the Escort Section were playing cards in the mess when a loud explosion was heard outside. Cpl Keates and three other members of the section armed themselves and took a Land Rover to investigate. Seeing red tail lights disappearing into the distance, the team gave chase for about five miles but could not catch up with the vehicle. Returning to the residence, it was discovered that a tent about 100 meters from the house with a backup power generator inside had been damaged. On closer inspection, grenade fragments and blood were found nearby and it would seem that whoever had thrown the grenade did not bargain for the 'trampoline' effect of the grenade striking the tent and bouncing back causing untold injuries to the thrower.

In the midst of all the trouble in 1956, LCpl Parry was posted to Famagusta in Cyprus and assigned as a member of Brigadier JAR Robertson, Bde Comd, 51 Inf Bde Escort Section. The Brigadier was described as a gentleman, who always ensured the Section was always catered for when he had social engagements of his own. Although the Bde Comd always looked after the escorts, on one occasion they were tasked with taking him to Kantara high in the mountains, not regarded as a safe environment for a high ranking British officer. In the middle seemingly of nowhere, the Brigadier orders the driver to stop, jumps out of the car and proceeds to the boot of the car, where he produces a gardening trowel and some flowerpots. Under the protection of LCpl Parry and his team, who, themselves, feared being shot at any moment, the Bde Comd spent a pleasant time digging up plants before replanting them in the pots. All ended well with a safe return home.

In 1958, Cpl Douglas Austen was enjoying a posting with 227 Provost Company in Larnaca, Cyprus, thinking life was good and awaiting his second stripe at any minute. As was often the case in those bygone days, opportunities were few and far between, but when they did present themselves they tended to leap up at you and LCpl Austen found himself packing his bags in short order and moving to Episkopi to be part of Lt Gen Sir Roger H. Bower, K.B.E., C.B. C-in-C MELF Escort Section. The General was a keen supporter of the RMP and would have no other soldiers as his escort (although the outer perimeter security of the residence was now provided by members of the Royal Artillery). The section was commanded by a Company Sergeant Major (CSM) and joined by 4 Corporals and

13 Lance Corporals, including LCpl Royton Oswick RMP, who arrived straight from training at the RMP Depot Training Establishment at Inkerman

Barracks Woking.

The escort section was accommodated under canvas and the duties rotated through guarding the gate of Flagstaff House, the home of the General now in Paralimni a few miles from the Episkopi Garrison HQ, and escorts to both C-in-C and his wife and family.

The escort vehicles used were Land Rovers, and although Close Protection developed into quite a low-key affair, in those days it was normal to display a show of strength with the bumpers highly polished, wheel discs fitted and a high level of shine all round. The vehicles were stripped down with all canopies and top doors removed with the ability to mount a Bren gun to the front with 200 rounds of ammunition. With the added risk of decapitation by wire placed across the road by EOKA, a long piece of angle iron was welded vertically to the front of the escort vehicles in order to break the wire. The General would travel in his official car, a huge black Austin Princess driven by an NCO from the RASC. When escorting the General, he would sit in the rear of his car with the WO2 in the front passenger seat and the two Land Rovers, each with 4 NCOs, at the front and rear of the flag car. Over the period of the campaign NCOs carried a variety of different weapons; .38 Webley revolver with 20 rounds, Smith & Wesson revolvers and 9mm Browning semi-automatic pistols, Sterling sub- machine guns with 60 rounds of ammunition and Thompson 'Tommy' sub-machine guns in canvas bags. Combined with the continued support of the Bren guns and boxes of smoke grenades, (that looked like 'Brasso' tins'), the teams had what was considered in those days as quite an arsenal.

There was an incredible sense of pride within the section that followed the Corps Motto 'Exemplo Ducemus', (*By Example Shall We Lead*), to the letter. Being in the spotlight continuously, routine dress inspections became redundant as the turn out and bearing of the NCOs was exceptional and the cause for much competition. Although the hours were long, the camaraderie that existed between the NCOs lifted spirits on difficult days.

The competition migrated to that of the GOC's Escort Section, also RMP, and whenever one section visited the other the vehicles were never left unattended, as both would try to recover a 'souvenir' from the other with wheel trims being fair game.

The relationship between the General and the section was one that is typical (even today) with Christmas dinner being served to the section in Flagstaff House by the C-in-C and the Sergeant Major. Gate duty on Christmas Day was provided by a young Captain from The King's Own (Yorkshire Light Infantry), who was appointed as ADC to the General and no doubt volunteered for the task to keep spirits up. On another occasion, LCpl Austen recalls that six of the Section were to escort the General and his family to the heights of the Troodos Mountains, where they believed a very cold time was to be spent keeping watch. Upon arrival, the General directed the team to the NAAFI and told them to kit themselves out in winter gear. They subsequently enjoyed a very pleasant winter break with the C-in-C and his family; all expenses paid! LCpl Austen left the services in 1959 and, as with so many members of the Escort Sections and the wider CP fraternity, holds such memories dear.

With the cessation of EOKA activities on the 9th March 1959 the Escort Sections were disbanded. However, throughout 1961/62, a section of 6 NCOs under the command of WO2 Barker RMP again provided the service to General Sir Dudley Ward, GOC Middle East with LCpl Michael Foster supporting the section as a dog handler from 6 Dog Coy RMP. Close Protection of Generals continued after this with 'operators' being provided by the Cyprus-based Provost Company. It is likely that this was the first time the term 'Close Protection', now CP, was used.

Circa 1954/55, Cpl Aldworth (from the spinning Jeep incident) was serving in Hohne, Germany, and was charged with escorting GOC 2 Div Maj Gen Basil Coad CB CBE DSO & Bar[13], whilst he visited 45 Field Regiment Royal Artillery (who along with the GOC had seen action during the Korean War) as they trained on Hohne Ranges. The troops were practicing a creeping barrage[14] and after parking his Land Rover in a hollow on the range floor, Cpl Aldworth escorted the General (with entourage) forward to observe the bombardments of the next ridge. At this time, the shells were being fired from behind over the heads of the VIP party and landing a few hundred metres away (not something that would be practiced today!). As the VIP group looked on, a 25Ib shell fell among the vehicles in the hollow to the rear. One soldier was badly injured and although the VIP party and escorts were unscathed a piece of flying shrapnel narrowly missed Cpl Aldworth's leg. The Land Rover was peppered with shrapnel damage and Cpl Aldworth's helmet, on the front

---

13   Major General Basil Aubrey Coad CB CBE DSO & Bar (27 September 1906 – 26 March 1980) was a senior British Army officer. He held battalion, brigade and divisional commands during the Second World War and immediately after, but is best known as the Commander of 27th British Commonwealth Brigade during the Korean War.

14   A creeping barrage was a bombardment of an area before the advancement of troops into it. The barrage would then move further towards the enemy, each time troops would move forward into the newly bombarded area and so on.

seat, also took a hit. The General looked round at the scene of the explosion, then carried on watching the shells that were landing in the right place. It transpired that a Gunner had not changed the range of his gun. Hohne ranges are notoriously dusty with black sand everywhere and following the explosion the escorts were covered head to foot. After scrounging a lift on a Bren Gun Carrier (an open top tracked vehicle), the party returned to Hohne Garrison, where Cpl Aldworth was met by Lt Walker RMP, who promptly put him on a charge for his state of dress. How things have changed!

The relationship between Close Protection and LCpl Oswick did not end there. On being posted to 101 Pro Coy in Dusseldorf, LCpl Oswick spent time at the 'Depot', (colloquialism for the RMP Training Centre that continues today), and whilst on duty as Guard Commander his CP background was noted. In short order, he was in front of the RSM, WO1 Mullinder, who informed him that the Corps was moving into the field of Close Protection and formal training would be required for volunteers and that a training unit would be formed at RAF Tangmere near Chichester. LCpl Oswick was promoted and, given his previous experience in Cyprus, was tasked with planning the training. The first hurdle was to be Police Advanced Driving Course conducted at Hendon followed by a Close Protection Officers Train the Trainer course both conducted by the Metropolitan Police. On his return, Cpl Oswick planned the first course, and after the programme was ratified by the RSM and Commandant, the first official RMP CP course was conducted in the autumn of 1961.

At the time the majority of special overseas CP duties were carried out by the SAS and the decision was made to send CP Instructors on the Special Forces Training Course at Hereford to establish if they were up to the task. After completing Parachute Regiment training at Aldershot, a rather bewildered Cpl Oswick found himself on the course at Hereford, which he subsequently passed, (and deployed with them on a number of unrelated operations),returning to Tangmere and the course. As is often the case with these ventures, higher military command decided the cost of the course was too expensive and it was duly cancelled. No sooner had it been cancelled, Cpl Oswick was back in Germany.

The Corps quickly recognised the need for Close Protection and it was started up again in Germany and Cpl Oswick was selected to travel to all the RMP companies worldwide to identify suitable candidates for training. This it would seem was another cost saving measure, as it was far cheaper to send one NCO around the world, rather than many would be candidates travelling to Germany, some of which would not be successful. Cpl Oswick continued to work within the CP environment throughout his 23 years service with the RMP and finished his career as a WO1.

In the 1960s, trouble was also brewing in the Middle East with an increasing insurgency against British Crown forces in the eastern and southern parts of what is now Yemen on the southern Arabian Peninsula. By 1963 and in the ensuing years, anti-British guerrilla groups with varying political objectives began to coalesce into two larger, rival organizations: firstly, the Egyptian-supported National Liberation Front (NLF) and, secondly, the Front for the Liberation of Occupied South Yemen (FLOSY), who attacked each other as well as the British. These attacks culminated on 10 December 1963, when the NLF carrying out a grenade attack at Khormaksar Civil Airport against Sir Kennedy Tevaskis, the British High Commissioner. As a result of the attack, a woman was killed instantly and the High Commissioner's assistant, George Henderson, who placed himself between the grenade and the High Commissioner, died of his injuries some days later.

It was as a result of this attack that the British Government declared a state of emergency in the British Crown Colony of Aden, a British possession since 1837, and its hinterland, the Aden Protectorate. For the first time a joint service police 'unit' came under one command. Consisting of 27 RMP, 2 WRAC Pro[15], 2 WRAFP[16] and 4 RN regulators, who provided limited policing, (being restricted as Aden was on a war footing with very limited in-bound areas for servicemen and women off base), provided guards for the service ambulances as well as responding to terrorist incidents and Escort Duties. Included in the teams were A1 Leading Seaman Sandy Saunders, Cpl Bob Campbell RAFP, Glen Craigie and Cpl Dennis Jobling. On a number of occasions the 'Joint Service Police' would be requested by the High Commission to escort arms and ammunition 'up country' to what were believed to be loyal Arab tribes only to find them a short time later in the hands of terrorists in Aden.

---

15 In 1948 the Secretary of State, Mr Emmanuel Shinwell, made a formal submission to the Crown for permission to raise a Corps of Women for the Regular Army and Territorial Army. This received the Royal Assent on 1 February 1949 the Women's Royal Army Corps (WRAC) came into being. For the first time women in the army became subject to all sections of the Army Act. Dame Mary Tyrwhitt DBE TD was the first Director of the WRAC.
16 The Women's Royal Air Force was formed on 1 April 1918. At the same time, the Royal Flying Corps (RFC) and the Royal Naval Air Service (RNAS) came together to form the Royal Air Force (RAF). The WRAF included volunteers from the Women's Army Auxiliary Corps (WAAC), Women's Legion drivers and the Women's Civilian Subordinates.

Provost NCOs were also called upon to escort suspected terrorists from and to Bedouin Legion outposts but the use of a RAF DC3 subdued the suspects as many had not seen let alone flown in any form of aircraft..

The threat against British military commanders was extremely high and the deployment of escorts fell to the Joint service Provost Unit commanded by A/Capt Colin Watkins. Enhanced weapon training took place for all NCOs on the ranges close to the RAF Provost and Security Service (P&SS) HQ. (40 P&SS consisted of the Joint Services Provost Unit – SIB, RMP and Counter Intelligence and RAF personnel.) Although all service policemen, the team make-up was dependent upon the principal. For example, the GOC would have two RMP plus two 'others and the C-in-C would have two RN plus two others. The drivers often carried a .38 Smith and Wesson revolver with the team carrying Sterling Sub Machine Guns (SMGs). The team would carry two cut down magazines that had been adapted by the REME armourer in order to facilitate movement in confined places. Two standard magazines (each containing 28 rounds) were carried in pouches. Colin Watkins recalls 7.62mm Self Loading Rifles (SLRs) were also available. However, the threat was mainly localised gunfire or grenades from side streets and the SLR with its long range would have been excessive with the risk of collateral damage too great. Except the C-in-C, who liked his limousine, the teams travelled in Mini cars and Land Rovers with chicken wire instead of a canvas canopy and angle iron projections to protect from piano wire stretched across roads. The escort teams to the C-in-C used open-top Land Rovers with no doors or tail gates with the rear compartment covered with wire netting to defend against grenades thrown by terrorists and to allow those 'successful' grenades to be kicked out or rolled out through acceleration, which made for very quick thinking crews, (Cpl Jobling had grenades thrown at him four times!). On the arrival of a VIP, briefings were given dependent upon the situation before moving from the airhead. Protection was provided to the respective GOCs, including Maj Gen Sir Michael Carver, Maj Gen Sir John Willouhby and Maj Gen Philip Tower, (who was very protective of his escort team), on a regular basis, the Commander-in-Chief, General Sir Charles Henry Pepys Harington[17], C-in-C

---

17 General Sir Charles Henry Pepys Harington GCB, CBE, DSO, MC (1910 – 13 February 2007) was an officer in the British Army. He served in the British Expeditionary Force and in Normandy in the Second World War. He was later Commander-in-Chief of the three-service Middle East Command from 1963 to 1965, based at Aden. He ended his Army career as Chief of Personnel and Logistics at the UK Ministry of Defence from 1968 to 1971.

Lt Col Colin Campbell Mitchell (driving) an open topped
Land Rover in the Crater, Aden 1967.

ME Admiral Sir Michael Le Fanu[18], (who, on occasions, after dark, would travel in the rear of the Land Rover posing as 'shotgun' with the team with one of his junior members of staff travelling in the staff car).

On June 20, 1967, there was a mutiny in the South Arabian Federation Army, which also spread to the police. Order was restored by the British in Operation Stirling Castle, mainly due to the efforts of the 1st Battalion Argyll and Sutherland Highlanders, under the command of Lt-Col Campbell Mitchell[19], but not before the loss of 23 British soldiers.

There are many tales to come from Aden but one which the reader may appreciate is remembered by Cpl Jobling and reflects upon the type of person the RMP are often called upon to protect.

> An incident comes to mind that, during the General Strike, we had to meet the GOC in Maalla to escort him to Sheik Othman. This just so happened to be the day of torrential rain and we had difficulty starting our car. Eventually the MT Corporal got us going and Sandy drove like a mad man to meet up with the GOC. As we were driving up Maalla Main Street, the General was coming in the opposite direction. With some nifty driving, Sandy about-turned and we eventually caught up with him. We then escorted the GOC

---

18 After junior officer's training, Admiral Le Fanu spent three years in destroyers, before qualifying as a Gunnery Officer in 1938. Le Fanu was promoted to Admiral in 1965, and became Joint Commander of the three services in the Middle East. for one year, during the period of British evacuation from the area. In October 1970, he was about to take over as Chief of the Defence Staff, when serious illness prevented this, and he retired at the age of fifty-six with the rank of Admiral of the Fleet. He died in London a month later on 28th November.

19 Lt Col Colin Campbell Mitchell (17 November 1925–20 July 1996) was a British Army lieutenant-colonel and politician. He became famous in July 1967 when he led the Argyll and Sutherland Highlanders in the British reoccupation of the Crater district of Aden. At that time, Aden was a British colony and the Crater district had briefly been taken over by nationalist insurgents. Campbell became widely known as "Mad Mitch". His reoccupation of the Crater became known as "the Last Battle of the British Empire". Although some observers questioned whether the Last Battle was ever worth fighting, the event marked the end of an era in British history and made Mitchell an iconic figure.

British Army Wall Chart of the Sterling L2A3

out across the Isthmus to Sheik Othman. It was here that FLOSSY and the NLF were having a battle with the security forces. Gen Willoughby halted his vehicle about 400 metres from the town's outer wall and stood up in his seat and began to film the battle with an 8mm camera. We had taken up the practiced security position of 4-quarter defence, two men at the front of the General's vehicle and two behind. I was placed at the General's rear. By this time, rounds were flying in our direction and the General began to berate me about opening fire without his permission. This was said while he was tapping my head with his baton. I politely informed him that I had not opened fire but the other side was shooting at us, at which point the General sat down and took off like a bat out of hell towards the Anglian line that was having the fire fight. We stayed there for four hours until we were able to move to again.

It is certainly true that Military Commanders, who have had the benefit and continue to enjoy the company of RMP protection over the years, are of a certain ilk and generally all live in a world of perceived indestructibility.

Tours typically lasted two years and, although Aden was an extremely unpleasant place to be, it is interesting that the troops had the opportunity to visit a cinema at HMS Sheba where films such as *Carry On Screaming* could be enjoyed or spirit-lifting music could be heard being played on Aden Forces Radio or the British Forces Broadcasting Service by Sarah Kennedy, who, until

THE EARLY YEARS 53

Commonwealth War Graves at Silent Valley cemetery, Aden. (Photograph taken in 2003 by Cpl (later SSgt) Micky McLean RMP)

recently, was still spinning discs on BBC Radio 2.

Following the lowering of the Union Flag without pomp or circumstance at RAF Khormasker in November 1966 by the British High Commissioner and Maj Gen Sir Philip Towers and his escort section, including Cpl Dennis Jobling and SSgt (later Capt) Colin Whatman, the VIP party were the last British servicemen to leave what was once the British Protectorate of Aden on the 29th November 1967. No ceremony was held and the VIP party flew to Bahrain and, dressed in desert shorts and summer shirts, were met with freezing weather and snow on returning to the United Kingdom.

As is the case today, the RMP would join forces with other Commonwealth Military Policemen to provide escorts throughout large visits. Cpl Jim Barnes was a National Service Military Policeman between 1958 and 1960 before joining the Australian army. In 1965 Cpl Barnes was serving with 28 Comwel Infantry Brigade Group at Terendak Army Camp, Malacca in Malaysia, when he and members of the RMP and New Zealand Military Police were called upon to provide an escort to the Duke of Edinburgh, HRH Prince Philip during his state visit (below).

It wasn't only the theatres abroad that saw the employment of service policemen as VIP escorts. In 1960, whilst enjoying National Service, ex LCpl David Davies was stationed at London District RMP and, together with members of the RAF, provided VIP escorts throughout the Royal Tournament held at Earls Court annually. The RMP and RAFP were billeted at Earls Court and with two performances of the show a day were kept extremely busy by visiting VIPs, most notably Her Majesty the Queen, King Saud of Saudi Arabia, and the then British Prime Minister Harold McMillan and Field Marshal Lord Montgomery. LCpl Davies recalls that when Lord Montgomery

HMA Mr. Michael Gifford laying a wreath at the Cross of Sacrifice, Maala Military Cemetery, Republic of Yemen, on Remembrance Day.

Members of the RMP and New Zealand Military Police providing escort to the Duke of Edinburgh, HRH Prince Philip, Malacca, Malaysia 1965.

Walther PPK 7.65mm: Length 155mm – Weight 590g – Muzzle velocity 308 m/s – Effective range 40m.

arrived at Earls Court he was escorted by a further three 'redcaps' and two RAFP 'snowdrops' and was seen to his seat without a hitch. The end of the evening saw a different story with only LCpl Davies and LCpl Brocklehurst RMP being the only two members of the escort part to turn up to see 'Monty' to his car. There was much adulation for Montgomery but there were also those members of the public, who posed a genuine threat to him, so the walk through the mêlée following the end of the performance was quite interesting and confirmed the place of the two LCpls in the annals of close protection. What happened to the remaining escorts remains a mystery but all ended well.

RMP support of the civil authorities including Special Branch continued and in1976, WO2 (later Major) Geoff Harland was appointed as the Warrant Officer in charge of the protection detail assigned to Princess Margaret during a whistle stop tour of Cyprus. The relationship between the RMP and the Royal Family continued and in 1977, HM Queen Elizabeth, having graciously agreed to be the Colonel-in-Chief of the RMP in that year, visited the Royal Military Police Training Centre (RMPTC), Roussillon Barracks in Chichester. Not only was it the Queen's Silver Jubilee year but also the Corps centennial[20]. Dressed in a three piece suit and sporting long hair and a Zapata moustache, (common with CP operatives of the day), Sgt Pete Glover RMP was charged with providing Close Protection to Her Majesty, supporting Commander Michael Trestrail, of the Royal Protection Department of the Metropolitan Police Service and the Queen's Principal Protection Officer. Under normal circumstances this style of moustache would contravene Queen's Regulations as the hair extended below the lower lip and the hair on the head longer than

---

20 On 1 August 1877, the Military Mounted Police was formerly established as a distinct Corps for service both at home and abroad, and it is from this date that the RMP claims its current place in the British Army's modern 'Order of Battle'.

would normally be tolerated. However, the need to blend in with the fashion of the day worn by civilians outweighed the risk of potential wrath from a trenchant RSM. Sgt Glover was armed with a 9mm Browning pistol secured (with a round in the chamber) in a shoulder holster with a spare magazine of 12 rounds in his jacket pocket. The weight of the magazine helped with clearing the jacket away from the holster in the event a quick draw was required. It was Special Branch protocol for their officers to wear their suits buttoned up, which impeded the draw of a concealed weapon. However, whether myth or otherwise, it was believed that Commander Trestrail regularly carried an umbrella that was designed to conceal a firearm, in this case a Walther PPK 7.65mm. Also accompanying the Queen was General Peter Leng, KCB, MBE, MC, Colonel Commandant of both the RMP and RAVC, Lt Col Mike Plewman, Commandant RMPTC and Provost Marshal (Army) (PM(A)) Brig Mike Mathews MBE[21]. On a side issue, the Queen had been presented with a silver broach, encrusted with diamonds depicting the Corps badge earlier that day. The day passed without incident, but is firmly entrenched in the History of the RMP. In the same year, Sgt Glover also provided discreet protection by posing as a photographer to Sir Robert Mark[22], whilst he visited RMPTC to review the troops.

The RMP continued to provide this capability until the political climate changed and the focus of UK operations became less global, instead centering on issues at home, the most notable of which was the situation in Northern Ireland, known as the 'Troubles'. Following the bombings of Hyde and Regents Parks as well as some Tube stations by the Irish Republican Army (IRA), it was believed that the Commanding Officer of the Irish Guards based at Chelsea Barracks was a target on an IRA hit list. Sgt Bob White and Cpl Andy Mudd were tasked to his home in order to provide close protection for both the CO and his wife. Unusually for the team who were operating without civil police, the CP team were given authority to carry firearms. The team remained in place for two weeks without incident.

---

21 Brig Mathews was commissioned into the King's Royal Rifle Corps and was Platoon Commander in the Long Range Desert Group during the Second World War before transferring to the Bays in 1947. He joined the RMP in 1961.
22 A former police officer, who served as Chief Constable of Leicester City Police, and later as Commissioner of the Metropolitan Police from 1972 to 1977, and was the first Metropolitan Commissioner to have risen through the ranks from the lowest to the highest, a route followed by all subsequent Commissioners.

Chapter 2

177 (Support) Pl Northern Ireland (OP BANNER)

Partition of Ireland in 1920 saw the eventual foundation of the Republic of Ireland (RoI) and Northern Ireland (NI). As such, Northern Ireland retained a military presence in line with the rest of the United Kingdom and Units forming 39 Inf Bde in Lisburn, were dispersed throughout the Province and 173 Pro Coy RMP, with its HQ based in Thiepval Barracks, Lisburn provided Provost support.

During the 1960s, discrimination in Northern Ireland against the Catholic minority had become institutionalised. In addition, the Province was in some economic difficulty. In 1963, Capt Terence O'Neil, the Prime Minister of Northern Ireland introduced measures to improve the economy but realised that he also had to address the simmering social and political issues. He met with the Republic of Ireland's Prime Minister and sought opinion from the nationalist communities in the Province. This caused unrest amongst the Unionist community. With Catholic hopes raised on one side of the community and Unionist fears on the other, violence finally erupted in 1966, following the 50th anniversaries of the of the Battle of the Somme and the Easter Rising – touchstones for Protestant and Catholic communities respectively. Rioting and public disorder eventually led to the murders of two Catholics and a Protestant by the 'loyalist' terror group, the Ulster Volunteer Force (UVF). Despite new initiatives being introduced by O'Neill, many Catholics were not content with the pace of reform and remained unconvinced of the Prime Minister's sincerity. The result was the founding of the Northern Ireland Civil Rights Association (NICRA) in 1967, which called for the end to injustices ranging from council house allocations to fair elections.

Peaceful civil rights marches continued until one eventually descended into violence in October 1968 when marchers in Londonderry defied the Royal Ulster Constabulary (RUC) and were dispersed with some aggression. O'Neill's reforms failed to deliver on NICRA's demands and after a brief cessation, the civil rights marches continued with the RUC responding in the same heavy-handed fashion. Following an election and against a backdrop of violence, O'Neill's replacement, James Chichester-Park, opted to continue with his predecessor's reforms. However, paramilitary groups from both sides of the sectarian divide began to operate and civil rights marches became more confrontational. Following the annual Apprentice Boys' march in August 1969, civil unrest in Belfast led to three days of nationalist rioting in Londonderry. The 'Battle of Bogside' only ended when, at the request of Chichester-Clark, the 1st Battalion the Prince of Wales' Own Regiment of Yorkshire, deployed in support of the RUC on the 14th August 1969. Despite political attempts to resolve the nationalist issues, violence continued, particularly with Loyalist attacks on Catholic areas escalating and many homes being burned.

The Irish Republican Army (IRA), which wanted a unified socialist Ireland, remained largely inactive during this period. It had stopped its campaign of border violence in 1962, having been suppressed by the actions of both the RoI and NI authorities. In late 1969, the 'Provisional' IRA (PIRA) broke away from the 'Official' IRA with the aim of using violence to achieve its aims. Loyalist paramilitaries were also becoming more organised. In late August 1969, the Northern Ireland government made a formal request to the UK government for military reinforcements to support the RUC throughout and OP BANNER[1] was initiated.

Major 'Jock' Lindsay RMP was in command of 173 Pro Coy RMP in 1969 and also held the staff appointment of Deputy Assistant Provost Marshal (DAPM) within Headquarters Northern Ireland (HQNI). As DAPM, he was assigned Cpl (later WO1) Eddie Monks to be his clerk. Cpl Monks had transferred to RMP from the Grenadier Guards and had no clerical experience. However, given his infantry experience and with the violence in Northern Ireland increasing, the DAPM assigned Cpl Monks to the General Officer Commanding Northern Ireland (GOCNI), Lt Gen Sir Ian Freeland GBE, KCB, DSO, DL[2] to be his personal bodyguard. Cpl Monks readily took on the task, albeit with no formal training, and accompanied the GOC on a daily basis throughout the Province.

By early 1970, Provost Branch HQNI had increased its establishment and now comprised an Assistant Provost Marshal, Lt Col Jack Thomas (later

---

1 Operation BANNER was the British Armed Forces operation in Northern Ireland between August 1969 and July 2007.
2 Gen Freeland had been appointed General Officer Commanding on 9 Jul 69 when just 1,000 soldiers were stationed there and subsequently gained the additional title of Director of Operations for security matters on 28th August 1969.

177 (SUPPORT) PL NORTHERN IRELAND (OP BANNER)

PM(A)) and a Staff Captain (Pro), A/Capt Colin Watkins (later Lt Col). A DAPM (Maj Brain Gait[3]) was appointed later the same year. 173 Pro Coy received OP BANNER reinforcements from the UK mainland and Germany and Pro Branch used this manpower to establish a Courts and Witness Section, an Arrest and Finds section and a Special Duties Section. During 1970 the MOD had assessed that PIRA, in particular, presented a threat to senior military officers within the Province, the UK mainland and in overseas garrisons and therefore directed that RMP should have formal responsibility for providing bodyguards and escorts to senior military officers where it was deemed necessary. The Special Duties Section would have responsibility for providing such escorts and bodyguards.

Cpl Colin Carnall MSM was posted to 173 Pro Coy in 1970 and, with his apparent skill with weapons, was assigned as bodyguard to senior military, political and civilian figures. Two vehicles were acquired for the role, Long Wheel Base Land Rovers, which had Macralon armour sheets attached for added protection. The additional weight led to extra carburettors being fitted to the engines, sadly this 'improvement' had little or no effect on the acceleration or top speed of 65mph.

For official functions two 'export only' Lincoln Continental cars were purchased. The first was white and allocated to the GOC; the second was black and allocated to Major General (later General) Sir Anthony Farrar-Hockley GBE, KCB, DSO & Bar, MC, who held the appointment of Commander Land Forces (CLF). Neither were armoured but could achieve 100mph. The section was armed with a Sterling Sub-Machine gun, a Browning pistol with customised serrated wooden pistol grips and feather light trigger, secured in a shoulder holster, and a 7.65mm Spanish Star semi- automatic pistol carried as a backup.

The Escort Section designed and produced 15 Heraldic Shields (shown overleaf), which depicted the two Cadillacs and the words 'Society Cohorts & bodyguards' (after the Praetorian Guard of Roman times) was inscribed in Latin. The shields were presented to the GOC, CLF, their staff and the team.

During these days of the 'Troubles', members of the Special Duties Section protecting such high profile appointments did not find everything went to plan: Whilst at Belfast Castle, the GOC made for an unexpected departure. In his haste to turn around, the driver of the General's car reversed too quickly

---

[3] Maj Gait was to go on to win the DSO as the Commanding Officer of one of the 2 RMP regiments to be raised during OP BANNER, to add to his DCM won with the Blackwatch in Korea.

One of the 15 original CP heraldic shields designed by the Escort Section.

and struck an old canon and carriage that was being used as an ornament. Typically in these scenarios, it was not simply a case of brushing off the damage and driving away. The car had hit the carriage in exactly the right spot and reversed up the canon lifting the rear wheels off the ground and leaving them spinning mid-air. It took a while to recover the vehicle but at least the GOC was rescued in short order … by the CLF!

In another incident, the resilience of the average RMP JNCO was proven beyond doubt. Late one evening outside Belfast City Centre, Cpl Carnall was approaching the junction of several roads when a radio message reported shots being fired. At the same time, an RMP Land Rover approaching from the left suddenly sped up, apparently responding to the radio message, and as it did so the rear doors burst open and with no tail-gate to stop him, an RMP LCpl fell out and momentarily laid in the middle of the road. After a few seconds he stood up, brushed himself down, turned and ran down the road after his vehicle, which luckily for him had stopped about 200 yards further on.[4]

The introduction of Op BANNER saw an increase in the establishment of military vehicles in the Province. Initially, Land Rovers as used by the Army in

---

[4] Cpl Carnall continued with the escort section until he was posted to Hong Kong and again assigned as bodyguard to the GOC, General (Later Field Marshal) The Lord Bramall KG, GCB, OBE, MC, DL, JP. Training alongside Cpl Rimmer RMP at the ranges on Stonecutters Island as well as the Hong Kong Civil police indoor range at police HQ did little to convince the General that he needed a bodyguard and, with a declining threat in theatre, he dispensed with the services of Cpls Carnall and Rimmer after eight months. Cpl Carnall returned to Chichester in 1975.

APM (NI) Lt Col (later PM(A)) Jack Thomas OBE, Brig N Davies PM(A) and Cpl Stuart Graham RMP with a BLMC Austin 1800

the UK and Germany were deployed and were eventually modified to be 'hard tops' with a Macralon outer layer applied. In addition, the 'civilian vehicle' fleet increased. From this initial fleet a BLMC Austin 1800 was chosen by Cpl Graham, who was tasked with the job of finding a suitable vehicle for bodyguard/escort duties by the Special Duties Section. The cars which were taxed and allocated a Northern Ireland civilian number plate were also issued military number plates, allowing them to be used whilst operating in either civilian clothes or uniform. The cars were also fitted with discreet storage for equipment and with two tone horns and blue lights which were discreetly fitted behind the front grill. This enabled the cars to be used as response vehicles; a fixture that has remained to the present day on vehicles used for Close Protection.

Movement throughout Northern Ireland by senior military officers and visiting VIPs was conducted on a daily basis by vehicle and helicopter. In the early days, in addition to the RAF helicopters, which came from RAF Aldegrove, the Army Air Corps (AAC) deployed personnel to Long Kesh on six month tours from Germany with Scout and Sioux helicopters. These helicopters would be replaced in later years by the Lynx and Gazelle. The GOC, CLF and Brigade Commanders would use the Scout helicopter on a regular basis whilst visiting VIPs and their ensuing entourage would be transported by the RAF in Wessex and Puma helicopters.

The Escort Section remained under command OC 173 Pro Coy until it was officially designated an Escort Platoon during the third quarter of 1971, when it was brought under the control of Pro Branch HQNI. On 5th November 1971, the Escort Platoon was reformed as a 2 platoon company (11 and 12 Platoon) and given the unit title of 177 Provost Company under the command of Capt Brian Wood RMP.

Members of the Company now included SSgt McNeil, Cpl Johnny Knock, Mal Harris, Bob Fuller and Cpl John O'Donnell, later RSM and founder of the Unit Investigation Element (UIE concept). The smallest and only 'all volunteer' company within the Corps, it comprised both GPD and SIB NCOs, who had little or no training in the specific role of body-guarding. 11 Platoon was responsible for providing manpower for the GOC[5] including Lt Gen Sir Ian Freeland, and later Lt Gen Sir Harry Tuzo GCB OBE MC (who implemented Op MOTORMAN[6]) and CLF, who both had a personal bodyguard and escort sections, and for Brigade Commanders[7], who were allocated individual bodyguards. 12 Platoon were responsible for providing bodyguards and escorts as required for military and civilian VIPs visiting HM Forces in Northern Ireland, which included the then Prime Minister, Edward Heath, who, whilst visiting soldiers of 8 Inf Bde at Christmas, was 'looked after' by Cpl O'Donnell. Prior to the formation of the RMP Courts and Witness Section, the platoon also had the responsibility of looking after individuals, both military and civilian, who were attending high profile or sensitive court hearings on behalf of the MOD.

Following the procurement of the BLMC Austin 1800, the company had by now increased its fleet of vehicles to include 3 Litre Ford Granadas, Cortinas, Vauxhalls and Austin Princesses, some of which were armoured. In addition, the Company also had Safari Land Rovers with Macralon armour, which offered very little protection against small arms fire. Apart from hand-held smoke grenades and a 38 web pattern haversack, containing a first- aid

---

5 The GOC lived in Cloona House, a Georgian Mansion on the outskirts of Dunmurry, Belfast, with Roman Catholic housing estates laying to the North and the South. The residence was protected by a section of infantry provided by the local unit, in whose TAOR the house sat.
6 After consultation with Whitehall, Tuzo saturated the republican areas of West Belfast and Londonderry with 30.000 troops and prized open the 'no go' areas. The success of OP MOTORMAN was a turning point in the troubles.
7 HQ 3 Inf Bde was in Lurgan, HQ 8 INf Bde in Londonderry and HQ 39 INf Bde in Lisburn.

Sgt John O'Donell RMP with Lt Gen Freeland (in centre front row) and other members of 177 Provost Company

kit, this was all the specialist equipment that was available. This said, a couple of NCOs did manage to 'acquire' canvas hammocks from the NI Ambulance Service, which served as improvised stretchers to be used in an emergency.

Dress of the day varied from light-weight trousers, standard army issue boots with putties, heavy duty pullover, combat jacket and a black beret with the RMP cap badge blackened. Members of the Company were also required to carry out their duties whilst wearing civilian clothes. This included casual clothing, which followed the fashion of the day from; Farah 'stay press' trousers, striped shirt, Corps tie, practical footwear and a skiing type jacket with go-faster stripes along the sleeves, to suits and even black tie with dinner suit. The discreet carriage of firearms in civilian clothes was essential and so shoulder holsters were issued, which required a cross draw. Most of the NCOs, however, preferred to purchase waist holsters, which fitted onto the trouser belt, in particular the 'pancake' holster, which was an American innovation and allowed the wearer to carry a pistol on his side of choice. The 58 web pattern holster, often referred to as a 'suitcase' due to the design, was used by NCOs,

Sgt John O'Donnell and team with Lt Gen Tuzo.

177 (SUPPORT) PL NORTHERN IRELAND (OP BANNER)

Sgt O'Donnell with the British Prime Minister Edward Heath and 8 Bde Comd, Brig JDF Mostyn MBE (later Gen Sir David Mostyn KCB CBE) in Londonderry 1973.

CP operators always look out, never in.

who would adapt them to their needs.

NCOs were issued with a 9mm Browning pistol and two magazines, one of which was carried in the pocket as there were no magazine holders available at the time. The Walther 7.65mm pistol was also available to NCOs. This weapon was ideal for concealment but lacked the firepower of the 9mm Browning and the magazine would only hold 7 rounds. For a support weapon, NCOs carried the SMG, which was the standard issue support weapon for the RMP. With two magazines taped together they would use them with the butt both folded and extended. In addition, some personnel were issued with the 7.62mm Self Loading Rifle (SLR). Despite its advantage of being an immensely powerful and accurate rifle, especially useful when Principals visited high risk areas, it was not a favourite among the team due to its overall length, which made it unwieldy and difficult to manage in a vehicle. It was not unknown for some NCOs to obtain the basic mesh vest that came as part of the Service Aircrew lifejacket, which with some alteration, provided a basic form of load carrying.

It became apparent that further training was required and, in order to improve weapon handling, members of the company, including the OC, Cpl John Knock and John O'Donnell were despatched to Hereford, where they attended a two week Close Quarter Battle Skills course with 22 SAS. A training regime was established and included First Aid, signals, walking drills, vehicle and building search and PT which included 'Kempa Katsumo', a form of defense and attack street fighting that relied upon a posture that did not give away your intentions, taught by Sgt John Brickwood, which was a form of defensive and attack street fighting, which relied upon a posture that did not give away your intentions. Selected NCOs also attended a Civil Police Advanced Driving Course back on the mainland. Additional First Aid training, which covered gunshot wounds, trauma management and CPR were given at the Medical Centre. Many Principals, who were new to the idea of protection, which was nearly all of them, were keen to take part in the training and were not averse to being 'manhandled' during anti-ambush scenario training. Those who were not so keen limited their participation to firing their personal weapon comprising of either a Browning or Walther pistol. Indeed, the NCOs involved in the early days of close protection made such an impression on the Commanders of the day that some of the original body-guards still receive Christmas cards from them today.

As 177 Pro Coy matured as a unit, it was widely perceived that it was full of 'rogues and vagabonds' and the likelihood is that it had more than

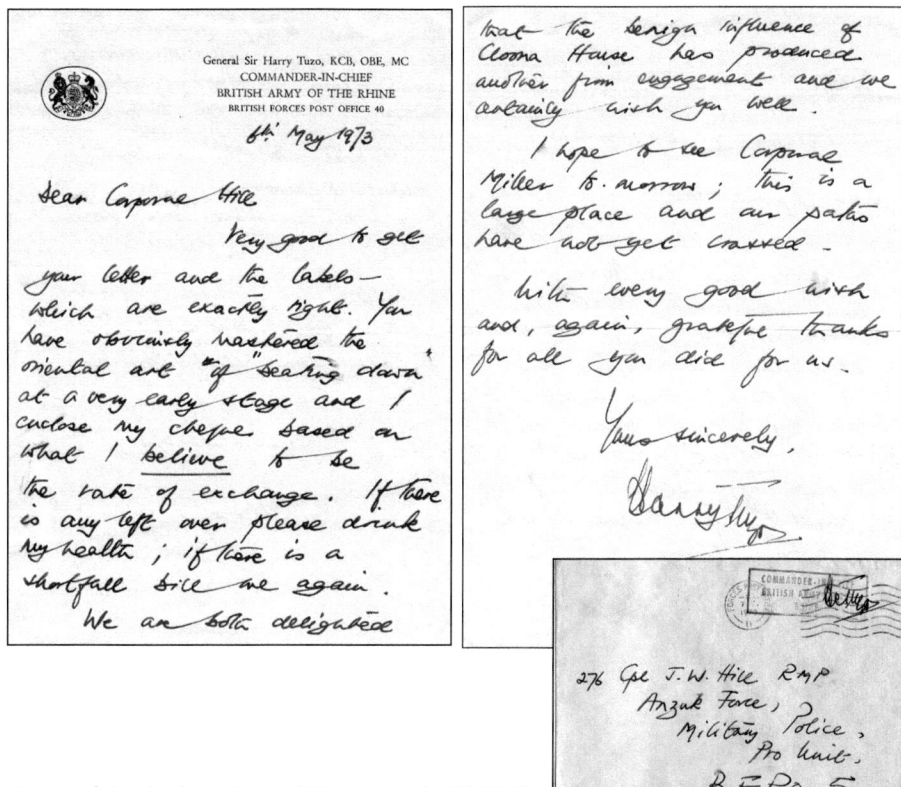

Letter of thanks from General Tuzo to Cpl Hill RMP

its fair share of colourful, outgoing personalities. It was, however, the kind of character that made for an excellent bodyguard as a less robust individual would not instil confidence in his VIP. For example, when on foot patrol with a Principal in areas such as Belfast, the CP teams quickly established a reputation of professionalism. The use of the 'Open Box' maintained the Principals image, whilst still maintaining security. Onlookers could see that the team were smart, alert ready to react. No incidents where the Principal came to harm ever occurred on such patrols. The personality of NCOs volunteering for the Company would be assessed and they would be required to undergo training within theatre, which would not only test their physical fitness, weapon handling and anti-ambush drills but also their ability to mix with senior officers and their families.

By 1973, the Company was now under the command of Capt John Allwood RMP with SSgt Carroll carrying out the role of CSM. 11 Platoon by this time had gained additional responsibility for providing bodyguards for the GOC and CLF and a UK Government representative, who was based in Holywood

Ex Cpl Ian Hay RMP (who had attended the RMP CP course in Werl in 1976) is seen here as a member of 177 Pro Coy in 1977. The British 7.62 Self Loading Rifle (SLR) had a muzzle velocity of 838 m/s and effective range in excess of 600m but with its length of 1.143m it was deemed too unwieldy for Close Protection duties.

on the outskirts of Belfast (the team were afforded lavish accommodation within his garage).

Both Capt Allwood and his successor Capt Arthur Liver RMP, both commissioned from the ranks and renowned as formidable RSMs, listened to the advice offered by their SNCOs when it came to identifying their replacements. SNCOs such as Sgt Pete Glover, NCO ic CLF Escort Section and Sgt Dave Cochran, NCO ic GOC Escort Section would be tasked if they knew of any suitable candidates, whose character and ability were conducive to the ways of the Company. If one was identified, he would be approached clandestinely and given an opportunity to accept or decline an offer to join 177. If a potential candidate agreed to a move, discreet action was set in place to have the posting authorized by the Manning and Records Office. The OIC Manning and Records Office would sometimes object to the posting on the grounds of career planning, but was always overruled on operational grounds.

In 1974, Sgt Dave Harding, Cpl Ken Blake, (Later Lt Col K Blake BEM), and four other NCOs attended the SAS bodyguard course at Hereford. The course curriculum, which included Walking Drills, Security Advance Parties (SAPs) and Residence Security Teams, (RSTs), was passed on to the remainder of the Company upon their return. Sgt Dave Harding is believed to have designed the concept of the 'quick draw' holster that is still in use today by many CP operators around the world. Cpl Blake moved to 3 Inf Bde in Lurgan as the Commander's bodyguard in February 1974, where he remained until March 1976. Other personalities who served with the Company until 1976 included Cpl (later Sgt) Pete Glover, John Bray, Frank Cambridge-King and Les Lander, who was later to attend the German Police Spezial Einsatz Kommando (SEK) Course in Berlin with Ken Blake in 1977.

By 1978, with the Company under the command of Captain (later to be PM(A)) IW Fulton, the GOC's team consisted of 6 NCOs, the CLF 5 NCOs and 9 NCOs provided CP for the 1 Star Commanders-in-Province, which by this time included the Brigadier holding the appointment of Chief-of-Staff HQNI. A VIP section was responsible for visiting VIPs and a Special Tasking Section provided support to the other sections in the form of SAPs and RSTs. Such tasks included providing discreet support to the CLFs bodyguard, whilst he accompanied the CLF in the Mourne Mountains at weekends, searching buildings such as Belfast City Hall and providing SAPs for the GOC when attending public engagements. The CS, WO2 John O'Donnell, identified a practical way to carry a large smoke canister beneath the car which could be detonated and dropped by means of a switch inside the car. The device was designed to be used in the event of an attack to allow either the personnel to deploy from the car or reverse away under cover of a smoke screen. Whilst the device was never used in anger – regrettably one NCO ignited the device and dropped it at the entrance of HQNI in the belief he was releasing the bonnet for the mandatory search!

The provision of bodyguards and escorts continued throughout the 1980s. With the establishment of the Close Protection Training Wing and subsequently the RMP CP Operations Wing, equipment evolved and became part of daily use in Northern Ireland, for example, the issue of the Heckler Koch 53, which remained in use until 2007. NCOs continued to attend the Police Advanced Driving Course as well as the in-theatre Team Medics Course. Many of the young NCOs, who earned their CP spurs with 177 Provost Company during this period, went on to serve with the RMP teams supporting the Foreign and Commonwealth Office.

Although the main threat was deemed to stem from dissident Irishmen and women, there were times when the CP team had to step in to counter different kinds of attack against the principal. In December 1983, it was reported in 'The Sunday World', a local Northern Irish newspaper, that whilst visiting Lisburn, the Duke of Gloucester was attacked by a dog, "Kludo", and that an SAS soldier intervened and saved the day. The soldier was in fact a RMP bodyguard named Sgt John Beck, whose nephew, Mick Dale, went on to join the RMP in the late eighties.

On 14th March 1984, an Ulster Volunteer Force (UVF) team from Rathcoole attempted to assassinate the then Sinn Fein Leader, Gerry Adams, following a visit to a Courthouse in Central Belfast, hitting him a number of times. The assailants made their escape by blending into the crowds on the busy streets surrounding Donegal Square and Queen Street. At the same time Cpl Andy Mudd, who was by now a member of 177, was conducting a recce of the Lord Mayor's Office when he heard the shots being fired …

> I was on a CP recce at the time, quietly going about my business at the Lord Mayor's Office. I was with the CP driver; trained guy from the Squadron in Lisburn, [Cpl] Steve Haughton. As we left the hall and drove past the Courthouse we heard the shots being fired and saw the brown Rover car that the gunmen were firing from. Was it us? Were they killing a policeman? Or was it SF taking out a terrorist? We were in civvies and had to make a quick decision to bug out or get involved. Steve was as keen as I was … so we sped after the car, chasing through the streets for a short distance only but going through traffic lights at red and screeching round corners. It was like Starsky and Hutch. Mentally, I thanked the Lord they didn't go straight up Grovernor Road into West Belfast. I had no time for the radio. Browning 9mm was out and cocked. Luckily, I hadn't chosen to take the Heckler Koch 53 with me, otherwise I would have to chase round in civvies with it. The terrorist's car came to an abrupt stop and also I noticed another car with a chap getting out, brandishing a nice shiny revolver. Steve stopped quickly and we got out and approached the brown car. I came up to the shooting position having seen the revolver … then the guy held out an ID card and shouted 'UDR!' … thank goodness I didn't shoot him. A chap was bleeding in the car having been shot by his own men, so Steve and I chased the two [now] running terrorists. Hoping to God we wouldn't be shot by trigger happy soldiers or policemen, we took one each of the guys, who were trying to look nonplussed and passive … no weapons in sight … Shouting and threatening, the guys were laid on their fronts and told not to move. Only then could we see they had masked faces and rubber-gloved hands. The crowds were gathered but luckily the RUC were close by and took them into the police station within minutes. A job done, we had to now calmly move the car blocking the traffic and get into the police station. Later, after informing Bde Ops who we were and why we were in civvies with weapons, the police told us what we foiled.

Whilst on a Close Quarter Combat course at the Long Range Reconnaissance School in Southern Germany, Cpl Mudd, (and Cpl Haughton), were awarded a Mention in Dispatches in the Autumn Operational Honours and Cpl Mudd finally received promotion to Sergeant before taking on the role as Training Sergeant. Joining Sgt Mudd at 177 were Paul Hancock, Paul

Evans, Ted Lockyer, Clive Hobson, Pete Irvine, Ray Massie, Roy Swayles, Nigel Davey, Pete Wilson, John Mudge, Alistair MacDonald, Gareth Own and Nigel Mears among others.

Towards the end of 1984, following a reorganisation of RMP in Northern Ireland, the Company was disbanded and became 177 (Support) Platoon of 175 Provost Company. In August 1987, following a further reorganisation, the platoon was placed under command of a reformed 173 Provost Company, which was now commanded by an SIB Major. The Company now comprised the Special Investigation Branch NI, (SIB NI), 177 (Sp) Pl and the Courts and Witness Section. The role of the platoon remained the same. However, a reduction in some specific tasks prompted a reduction in strength in the Province. Despite this reduction, the risks and threats that were inherent with working in such an environment were still evident. It must be remembered that the British Army was present in Northern Ireland to support the RUC.

In a cruel irony, the IRA continued to target serviceman in both Northern Ireland and mainland Britain and, in November 1989, they were successful in detonating a bomb under a car owned by (now) SSgt Andy Mudd, who had returned from a CP tour of Beirut a couple of months earlier and was now posted to Colchester with his wife Maggie.

> A couple of months of fitting in, career planning and routine GPD life came to a shuddering stop. Saturday 17th November 1989 about 10.30 a.m. Maggie and I jumped into our new [Volkswagen] Golf GTi to go shopping. Quick look under the body between our door posts, all clear. Then BOOM! It wasn't clear at all. The IRA had planted a bomb probably behind the front driver's side wheel. Small package, big bang. I remember everything. The slow-motion browning of the windscreen, the flash of fire tearing through the cab. The intense noise and heat. The smell of hot metal and plastic.
>
> I was thrust up at the roof and then fell back down. The front driver's door was gone and I went into ambush drill mode…Attack from the right …exit left. Instinctively I undid Maggie's seatbelt and pushed her to get her out. She screamed more from my appearance than for herself. Blood trickled down her face from a cut near her eye and her hand was burned. Luckily, that was it for her and by now two brave soldiers ran to the car and took her away. Fire was getting hold at the front and I was struggling to get my body over the gear lever.. I saw I had a big gash on my left thigh but no blood. My face stung with the heat within the car but everything else was just a dull

sensation. Shit … my hand had been shredded and a couple of fingers lost. The guys didn't come back for me. Not sure if I swore but I knew I just had to get out before the petrol tank exploded. By now I was in the passenger seat…rather lighter than I normally would be. I blocked the main obvious problem out. I never even thought about it. I waved at the two blokes again and luckily before I could drop on the floor the two blokes again came to my rescue. Lt Mike Simpson and Sgt Snookes were well-deserving of their Queen's Commendations for Bravery. The car was on fire ready to explode and they got me out. Training at once came to the fore. RMP first aid and the Combat Medic training for Beirut was what I knew. Lucky me, there was a young RAMC chap lived close by. He set to work on my groin…where my right leg used to be! Also he had to tourniquet the left leg as there was so much damage from foot to thigh. I could manage the elevation to the right hand and also by now I had delegated the 'keep me talking bit' to combat the shock to Charlie Tyler, a good RMP guy, who lived round the corner. I was dreaming of a nice ambulance with a proper doctor on board but to our horror there was an ambulance strike on and so all we got was two guys scratching their heads. Right you guys, you have to come with me… get this bloody thing moving…Still awake when the surgeon and his team were verifying details and cutting my best cords off and sticking needles in me. I remember saying to the main man [Andy Maye] you do your best to patch me up and I will do my best to stay alive. Oh, and keep this middle finger because I need to play golf again. Lots of blood and hours of surgery, then it was let's wait and see. Darkness, a tube down my throat to breathe and a little voice. 'If you can hear me, squeeze my hand.' Not Maggie's voice. It was the OC, Maj TP Watton. I was alive. Much weeping and wailing. Lots of well wishers. I was so glad I still had my wedding tackle: I wasn't bothered about anything else. That Douglas Baader moment came later. The rage, the bloody hell I have lost both. Why both? The right leg went at the scene. Ripped off at the hip landing in some poor sod's garden. The left leg had been damaged so much the surgeons elected to take it off just above the knee with a hope that the thigh wound would hold up to plastic surgery and possible prosthetic fitment. My dominant hand had lost two fingers and the middle one was now wired on with further surgery required. Burns and shrapnel wounds were just not worth bothering about. I was alive. Maggie was good and together we could get through this. Why me? Random and unfortunate. Me rather than the RAF neighbour. Worrying that it could

This photograph taken in 1986 shows members of 177 (Sp) Pl (including Cpl (later SSgt) Andy McMath 3rd from right) with the synonymous black berets and a 3 litre Ford Granada (The rifle is a Heckler & Koch 53 which remained in use until 2007 when it was replaced by the Diemarco C8)

have been Maggie on her own or even with relatives or friends. The IRA admitted planting the bomb and bizarrely apologised that it was me ... the man who caught the men who tried to assassinate Mr Adams.

Life in Northern Ireland was never dull and whether it was escorting a high ranking officer to Drumcree or flying low-level 'hedge hopping' from one County to another, excitement was never far away. Providing protection for a high-ranking military officer, even after the Good Friday Agreement, provided excitement that was, however, not without risk. On one particular visit the author provided protection for a visiting officer, who, at the end of his programme, flew from South Armagh to the tarmac of Londonderry Airport, the chosen aircraft being a Lynx helicopter. No seats, just a rope coiled on the shiny metal floor, a gunner looking out of the open door over the sights of his GPMG. The pilot let us know through head phones that a storm was coming in from the east and in order for us to reach our destination he would need to 'race' it staying at its very edge. The 'Boss' and I also needed to change

The threat in Northern Ireland was never far away. This is the result of a 500lb vehicle borne improvised explosive device that exploded in February 1998 on Edward Street in Portadown town centre. The device caused massive damage to shops and cars and the Real Irish Republican Army claimed responsibility. The photograph was taken by Cpl Paul Tyrer RMP who later became the Regimental Quartermaster Sergeant (RQMS) at the Close Protection Unit.

from uniform into civilian clothing for the onward journey. The storm came in and at one point it was as if you could reach out and touch it. The clouds were dark and in the distance lightening was flashing. The pilot flew from left to right and up and down as if negotiating a low level flight along an invisible canyon. The floor with no grip whatsoever, the ever-frantic change of direction and the open door all provided the most exhilarating change of clothes ever. Thankfully, neither the 'Boss' nor I tumbled out of the aircraft and after some incredible flying, we landed at Londonderry Airport, intact.

Later that year, Cpl Steve Carr RMP, was not so fortunate. At the time, he was the Close Protection Team Leader responsible for Comd 3 Inf Bde, Brig R M Brunt OBE based in Portadown. During his inaugural visit to 3 Bde, the Bde Comd hosted the newly appointed Deputy Chief Commissioner (DCC), of the RUC, Colin Cramphorn CBE, QPM, DL, FRSA, on a 'fly programme', visiting one of the mountain-top observation towers south of the town of Newry on the border with the Irish Republic in South Armagh. Since the closure of a vehicle check point nearby, the tower was critical in monitoring cross-border activity. The approach by air to the tower was regarded as extremely hazardous due to the topography; the aircraft would approach low, rise over the perimeter fence before dropping swiftly onto the helipad. Flying from RUC HQ in Knock, Belfast via HQNI, the aircraft had a full passenger manifest and the visit to the tower was the first serial on the programme. With top cover being provided by a second Lynx, the approach was made to the helipad of the tower. Climbing to approximately 30m above the perimeter fence, the helicopter suffered catastrophic mechanical failure and dropped onto the helipad, the rotors now disengaged from the gear box – lethal. Cpl Carr's own account of the crash emphasizes the pure professionalism of the RMP CP Operator and their ability to operate under extreme pressure:

> Believe me when I say it was a far more dramatic experience than was reported! The wait in the Lynx seemed like forever, but in reality it was probably only about a couple of minutes. We were very lucky that we dropped inside the perimeter of the tower, otherwise we would have hit the mountainside and slid all the way down, which doesn't bear thinking about. The atmosphere was extremely tense and the Load Master and I had to instill a level of calm to very panicked passengers, convincing them not to get out of the airframe (restraining some physically). The rotors were not under direct drive from the gearbox and would have proven lethal to anyone who had attempted an escape. I needed a calm yet forceful head on my shoulders to control the situation inside the aircraft.
>
> Due to the continued uncertainty of the weather and risk of breakdown, I had pre-positioned the Brigadiers armoured car and Close Protection Driver, LCpl John 'Fletch' Fletcher RLC at Bessbrook Mill, and the thought that was rushing through my mind at the time was, "How can I quickly regain control of this situation and get my boss to safety". Even as we hit the ground, and it was a hard hit, I was already thinking of Fletch at Bessbrook and how I would get him to my location.
>
> Following this near-death experience, once safely outside the downed aircraft, my recovery plan had already kicked-in, and when the Bde Comd asked me "What on earth are we going to do next?" I was able to give him an immediate, positive response as the wheels, so to speak, were already turning. I said to him words similar to, "You do your job and I'll do mine" and both he

177 (SUPPORT) PL NORTHERN IRELAND (OP BANNER)

and the DCC went to the briefing within the tower as planned. Never in my wildest dreams did I believe that the programme would go "no-fly" in such dramatic circumstances. Fletch literally put his head in the lion's mouth and drove, unsupported, from Bessbrook right into the heart of 'Bandit Country' to recover us, [the last British soldier killed during the 'Troubles' was based at Bessbrook, fatally wounded whilst operating a security checkpoint in 1997 by a sniper using a Barrett .50cal[8] rifle]. Although the journey would have been less than 10 miles, it was a truly heroic piece of driving that would normally have been banned under regular Army restrictions, as would the remainder of my no-fly plan.

When the briefing was finished, both the 'Boss' and DCC were able to travel by road, Fletch waiting for them as if that was always the plan. Leaving the rest of the party to fend for themselves at the tower, we completed the rest of the trip by road, operating in the most extreme Republican strongholds of South Armagh, such as Crossmaglen and Forkhill. We were self-sufficient, in that we did not call upon the Comd's Rover Group, [infantry support appointed to the Bde Comd for road moves in high risk areas], other Bde assets or the assistance of the host Battalions to support our road moves for the rest of the day. There simply wasn't the time or the opportunity to do so.

A short while later, the boss commented on how slick I was able to transition from a fly to a no-fly programme, with no disruption to the plan. He was clearly concerned that we had not followed conventional protocols that the regular army units would need to conform to, because if we did then the visit would have been stopped after the air disaster. His concern was balanced with the effectiveness of the no-fly plan, which enabled him to continue briefing the new DCC.

In Cpl Carr's annual report, Brig Brunt commented that he had, " … shown that he is an effective planner, who anticipates problems and makes sensible plans to overcome them". Cpl Carr continued to serve with the Bde Comd. However, on leaving the Royal Military Police after 13 years service, he was diagnosed with Post Traumatic Stress Disorder and this incident was one of eight life-threatening episodes that contributed to this. Cpl Carr still

---

8 The South Armagh Sniper is the generic name given to members of the IRA South Armagh Brigade who conducted a sniping campaign against British Security Forces from 1990 to 1997. The campaign is notable for the snipers' use of .50 BMG calibre Barrett M82 and M90 long-range rifles in some of the shootings.

78 DETER SUPPRESS EXTRACT!

Cpl Carr seen training at Ballykinler ranges.

receives support from Combat Stress[9] and Help for Heroes[10]. The crash itself was reported in local media some time afterwards.

Extract from the *Sunday Life* newspaper, Sunday 1st November 1998:

Top Cop in Copter Drama

The RUC's second highest-ranking officer was involved in a terrifying mid-air drama over Ulster's Bandit Country, Sunday Life can reveal.

RUC Deputy Chief Constable Colin Cramphorn and an army Brigadier were on board the Lynx chopper, when it got into trouble over South Armagh.

Only scant details of the September 30 incident were released by the Army and the identity of the passengers was kept a closely guarded secret.

Mr Cramphorn, the former Assistant Chief Constable of West Mercia, took up the post only in August.

The Lynx was preparing to land at an observation post at Cloghogue,

---

9   Combat Stress works with Veterans of the British Armed Forces, and members of the Reserve Forces, delivering effective treatment and support for mental health problems. www.combatstress.org.uk
10 Help for Heroes provides a national network of support for wounded servicemen and women and their families. www.helpforheroes.org.uk

outside Newry, when the pilot experienced handling difficulties.

Even though the lynx was near the ground, the incident was considered potentially life-threatening and the chopper was grounded.

Both DCC Cramphorn and the Brigadier completed their journey by road.

An Army spokesman confirmed on Friday that the lynx had a "serious engine fault", but refused to confirm who was onboard.

However, RUC sources confirmed that DCC Cramphorn and the Brigadier were among the passengers.

On the 30th October 1998, the 39 Brigade Commander, Brigadier (later General) Nick Houghton[11], was on his way to play Golf at Malone Golf Course when he observed strange goings on at the post office at Lambeg. He said something along the lines of "Blimey! The post office is being robbed, let's go!" Two masked men jumped into a getaway car and a third masked man wearing a combat jacket appeared in the doorway of the post office brandishing a Beretta pistol. When he saw the two plain-clothed soldiers jump from the Commander's car he dropped the gun and made good his escape in the waiting getaway car. At the scene the handgun was recovered and it was found to be an imitation. The RUC subsequently made a number of arrests. After the excitement, the Commander was concerned that he would be late for his game and so the team continued on their way. Sadly, as a result of the incident, the Rover 800, the Brigadier had been waiting six months for had been compromised on its first outing and was returned to the pool, to be replaced by a sunset orange Peugeot, which was not his favourite.

Although manning levels reduced over the years, 177 (Sp) Pl remained a critical element of the RMP mission in Northern Ireland. The Good Friday Agreement was the foundation of cessation of hostilities. Op BANNER finally ended on 31 July 2007 and with it the need for Close Protection in Northern Ireland. 177 (Sp) Pl finally disbanded that year.

---

11 General Sir Nicholas Houghton KCB CBE commissioned into the Green Howards in 1974 and commanded 39 Infantry Brigade in Northern Ireland from 1997 to 1999 and was the Director of Military Operations in the Ministry of Defence from December 1999 to July 2002. More recently, General Houghton was the Senior British Military Representative Iraq and Deputy Commanding General of the Multi-National Force-Iraq from October 2005 until assuming his appointment as Chief of Joint Operations at Permanent Joint Headquarters (UK) in March 2006. He became Chief of the Defence Staff in 2013.

INCIDENT DETAILS

'B' DIVISION

AT 1250 HRS ON 30.10.98 SONIA LESLIE WAS WORKING IN THE SHOP AREA OF LAMBEG POST OFFICE, 163 QUEENSWAY, LAMBEG. CLAIRE MURRY WAS WORKING IN THE POST OFFICE. THREE MALES WEARING BALACLAVA MASKS AND EACH CARRYING A HANDGUN ENTERED THE PREMISES. SONIA LESLIE WAS MADE TO LIE ON THE FLOOR AND HAND OVER £120 CASH FROM THE TILL. THE OTHER TWO ARMED MALES WENT TO THE POST OFFICE SECTION OF THE PREMISES AND SMASHED THE SECURITY SCREEN GLASS WITH A HANDGUN DEMANDING CASH. £4,500 WAS HANDED OVER BY CLAIRE MURRY. AS THE THREE MASKED MALES LEFT THE PREMISES THEY WERE OBSERVED BY AN ARMY PLAIN CLOTHES UNIT, WHICH STOPPED ON SEEING WHAT WAS TAKING PLACE. THE THREE MALES WERE SEEN GETTING INTO A GOLD VAUXHALL CAVALIER, ███████ WHICH WAS BEING DRIVEN BY A FORTH MALE. THE CAR DROVE OFF ALONG THE MOSS ROAD TOWARDS THE BELSIZE ROAD. TWO OF THE ARMY PERSONNEL GAVE CHASE ON FOOT AND DREW THEIR WEAPONS AND SHOUTED A CHALLENGE, NO SHOTS WERE FIRED.

A STEYER BB PISTOL WAS RECOVERED AT THE SCENE AND A BALACLAVA MASK WAS RECOVERED IN THE CAR PARK OF THE PREMISES. A SECOND MASK WAS FOUND AT THE JUNCTION OF THE MOSS ROAD/VENTNOR PARK APPROX. 1/4 MILE FROM THE SCENE. APPROX. £110 CASH WAS RECOVERED FROM THE SCENE, BELIEVED MONEY FROM THE TILL, DROPPED BY ONE OF THE ROBBERS. AT 1312 HRS THE VAUXHALL CAVALIER CAR, ███████ WAS RECOVERED CRASHED AT KERRYKEEL GARDENS, LENADOON. THIS VEHICLE WAS TAKEN BETWEEN 2000 HOURS AND 2300 HOURS ON 29.10.98 FROM ███████████████████████████████████████ A THIRD MASK WAS FOUND IN THE VEHICLE.

DESCRIPTIONS:

1. 5'9", GREY SWEATSHIRT, BLUE JEANS, SLIM BUILD
2. DRIVER - DIRTY BLOND HAIR, APPROX. 20/30 YRS OLD, SHORT DARK SCRUFFY HAIR AND A CHUBBY FACE
3/4 NO DESCRIPTIONS

ALL WORE BLACK BALACLAVA MASKS AND GLOVES AND CARRIED HANDGUNS.

3 SUSPECTS
1 CHARGED

Police report of incident details.

4 - THE STAR NOVEMBER 6, 1998

NEWS

POLICE ISSUE APPEAL AFTER GANG FLEES SCENE OF RAID AT LAMBEG

Soldiers pursue gang after post office hold-up

by FIONA MURRAY

PLAIN clothed soldiers attempted to stop a gang of armed robbers making a getaway after a post office hold-up last Friday.

Staff at Lambeg Post Office were terrorised by three masked men, each wielding hand guns, who burst in around 12.50pm and demanded cash.

But as the robbers fled from the Moss Road premises, the soldiers who were involved in a transportation run in the area, spotted them and pursued the gang on foot.

The gang then jumped into a waiting gold coloured Vauxhall Cavalier car, registration number EBZ 3203, where a fourth man was waiting.

This vehicle had been stolen earlier that day from the York Road area of Belfast.

The soldiers pursued the car but the robbers were able to escape with what police describe as a 'sum of money'.

Police say a BB gun, a mask and a small sum of money was later recovered at the scene.

A second mask was found at the Moss Road and a third recovered in the vehicle, which was later found crashed at Kerrykeel Gardens in the Lenadoon area of Belfast.

Lisburn police have issued descriptions of the four men involved in the robbery.

One was said to be of slight build, about 5'10" tall wearing a grey fleece jacket.

The second man was about 5'9" tall of slim build and wearing a grey sweat shirt and blue jeans and the third man was described as being between 20-30 years-of-age with dirty fair or blonde hair.

The fourth man is short, with dark scruffy hair and a chubby face. All were wearing black balaclavas and gloves.

Detectives at Lisburn are appealing for anybody who witnessed the robbery or noticed a gold coloured Cavalier acting suspiciously to contact them.

A police spokesperson said: "We are appealing to anybody who was in the vicinity of of McKinstry Road, Queensway, the junction of Moss Road and Queensway, Moss Road, Belsize Road, Wilmar Road and Stewartstown Road, between 12.30pm and 1.15pm last Friday and who saw the gold coloured car with four men on board acting suspiciously or being driven at high speed, to contact detectives at Lisburn CID."

The number to phone is 01232-650222 or use the Crimestoppers number on 0800 555111.

Article reported in *The Star* on 6 November 1998 regarding the robbery at Lambeg.

Chapter 3

British Army of the Rhine (BAOR), RTW Werl and UK

Before Close Protection was formalised, the SIB, who operated in plain clothes, were well-suited to the task at the time. Provided with unmarked, cars they provided protection when it was required until 1975 when GPD took on the task formally.

Stories of VIP escorts and Close Protection were not always about the threat of assassination or kidnap. In late 1953, whilst serving with 11th Armoured Div Pro Coy, the Escort Group to Maj Gen Pyman GOC, Sgt Bob Adams was escorting the General, who was travelling in a jeep with a staff officer, Lt Col D'Avigdore Goldsmid.1 The Colonel's black retriever dog was travelling with the escort section, themselves travelling in an open-top jeep. At a speed of approximately 45 mph, the intrepid hound decided it was far more interesting to travel with his master and leapt from the car completing a number of forward rolls before the backup car managed to stop and Sgt Adams coaxed him back into the jeep meeting up with the GOC at HQ. After explaining what had happened, the order was given for the escort jeep to be fitted with a steel chain dog lead.

On several occasions LCpl Alan Marsh was detailed to escort General Sir Richard Gale and other VIPs including Field Marshal Viscount Montgomery, General Dwight Eisenhower, HRH Prince Bernhardt of Holland and the Dutch Minister for War. Between 1955 and 1958, LCpl Marsh was posted to 101 Pro Coy RMP within HQ BAOR and, being the HQ, was extremely popular with important visitors. Marsh also escorted Marshal Alphonse Juin of France during a time of political unrest in his country. Juin bought his own chef, who would taste the food before serving it to ensure it had not been poisoned.

---

1   Major-General Sir James (Jack) Arthur d'Avigdor-Goldsmid, 3rd Baronet (19 December 1912 – 6 September 1987) was a British Conservative politician. He was a member of the prominent Anglo-Jewish d'Avigdor-Goldsmid family, and his brother Sir Henry d'Avigdor-Goldsmid, 2nd Baronet was also a Member of Parliament. Educated at Harrow School and then Sandhurst, d'Avigdor-Goldsmid became an officer in the British Army for 35 years. From 1963 he was Colonel of his old regiment, the 4th/7th Royal Dragoon Guards.

The visit of HRH Princess Mary to Bielefeld (LCpl Lumley is second in file from left)

On the Marshal's return to France, the RMP escort consisted of a Lieutenant, a Sgt as the driver, a Corporal and 5 LCpls all travelling in two Opel Kapitan cars with two German outriders. Armed with loaded .38 revolvers and Sterling sub-machine guns, which were known to go off if subjected to rough treatment or bumps in the road, all border controls were warned of the approaching dignitary and so the transit between Germany, Holland and France was very swift with the German outriders breaking off at the Dutch border. Alan recalls the Cpl asking the RSM before departure, "What if we get stopped for some reason?" The RSM replied, "Just open fire and ask questions later!" Such was the risk posed to Juin, who thankfully arrived in one piece.

In 1958, in her capacity as Colonel-in-Chief of 15th/19th The King's Royal Hussars, HRH Princess Margaret visited Münster, Germany. As they operated in civilian clothes and had civilian vehicles, 72 Section SIB stationed in Oxford Barracks were instructed by the DAPM SIB, Maj Ronnie Hughes to provide a 24 hour guard for HRH during her stay at the Commanding Officer's married quarter. With the CO's garage used as an 'ops room', (in reality a rest room) and three layers of protection were established: the outer being provided by the German Police including traffic control and dog patrols; the middle layer provided by RMP NCOs; and the inner being provided by members of 72 Section SIB. On the day, HRH arrived late at the house having visited the Lord Mayor of the local town and, after signing the visitor's book, her Special Branch protection officer handed over responsibility for HRH's safety to Maj Hughes. Soon afterwards HRH left for the Officers Mess (where it was rumoured the young officers could not keep up with the Princess and her dancing) and following an uneventful night, responsibility was returned to

Special Branch. Although brief, Maj Hughes received a letter of thanks from the Royal household and ensured that in the early days, the responsibility of CP fell upon the SIB.

Ex WO2 Brian Lumley was a LCpl serving in HQ 1(BR) Corps in Bielefeld and was called upon to form part of an escort group when HRH Princess Mary visited in October 1967. Led by Lt Keen RMP and Sgt Gentle in a 'jazzed' up military vehicle, LCpl Lumley, Sgt George Keith and two other JNCO formed a motorcycle escort to the VIP car as the Princess journeyed cross-country between garrisons. Although it often seems the life of a bodyguard is a glamorous one, this particular endeavour saw the escort group staying overnight in farmyard barns, which made cleaning their webbing a task in itself, not helped by the fact they were all wearing No 1 Dress ('Blues') for the duration of the visit.

As ex RSM SIB WO1 Brian Samways recalls he joined the Close Protection fraternity in the nineteen sixties and, with no holsters issued, his pistol was secured either in his waistband or pocket. He was instructed to purchase a trilby or German equivalent and that was that – you were kitted out for CP operations. In 1967, Brian was part of a team that travelled from Dusseldorf to Hohne in order to protect Her Majesty Queen Elizabeth II throughout her visit to the Royal Tank Regiment. Samways and his SIB colleagues continued to provide close protection to notable VIPS including Prince Berhard of Holland during his visit to Rheindahlen, Dr Borg Olivier, the Prime Minister of Malta, on his visit to the Royal Maltese Artillery based at Multiem-Ruhr, the Duchess of Kent when visiting British troops in Munster and Princess Anne when she visited her then fiancé, Capt Mark Philips.

With no formal close protection recognition at this time, RMP NCOs tended to dip in and out of the protection role. In 1970, ex Cpl Clinch, who was serving in 101 Pro Coy in Dusseldorf along with Cpl Mike Sutcliff and a SNCO, were all despatched to the British Ambassador's house where they were to secure the residence and ensure the safety of the then Prime Minister, Edward Heath, whilst staying overnight during a visit to Germany. Armed with only a 9mm Browning pistol, the only other protection the team had was a detachment of German police armed with machine pistols and Dobermans! If that line of defence had been compromised Cpl Clinch would have had a battle on his hands. However, the reward of an overnight stay in a nice hotel serving cold Kolsch beer made that risk all the more worthwhile.

As time went by, the continued commitment for Close Protection stayed with the SIB, although it was recognised that they still had no formal training for the task 'operating on a wing and a prayer'. However, being SNCOs and dressed in civilian clothing, they were well placed to fulfil the commitment. In 1971, Sgt (later Major) Geoff Harland RMP SIB was a member of an escort section charged with the protection of Princess Ann when she visited Mark Philips in Celle, and then in 1972, SSgt Harland was an armed escort to Edward Heath during his visit to Kiel in Germany.

In 1972 Cpl (later Captain) Steve Ketteringham, (known as 'Bones' to his friends), with an RMP officer, an Austin 1800 and two German police cars, escorted HRH Princess Alexandra, who was visiting the 17th/21st Lancers in Wolfenbütal, Germany. Although the Princess was staying at the home of 1 (BR) Corps Comd, she spent a very pleasant evening within the Officers Mess and on the return journey requested the escorts turn off the blue lights as she was feeling a little worse for wear. The news of the Princess' evening 'stayed in the mess' and Cpl Ketteringham escorted her for a further three days before she returned to the UK. 30 years later at a remembrance service held at the British Embassy, Bangkok, Cpl (now Mr) Ketteringham met the Princess once again and both he and the Princess enjoyed a short time reminiscing the times spent in Germany so many years before. Interestingly, that was not the end of Cpl Ketteringham's brush with Royalty. He also had the pleasure of escorting Princess Anne, whilst she powdered her nose while attending the Rhine Army Summer Show. This time though, he was armed with only a policeman's whistle. A force to be reckoned with and no mistake.

In 1974, it was recognised that the RMP mission in Germany did not have a specialist 'CP' section within theatre and PM BAOR, Col Bob Sherville (Late RMP), ordered APM 1 (BR) Corps, Lt Col Peter Stock MBE, RMP, to assume the responsibility for providing protection to visiting UK VVIPs to units in BAOR and the British Sector of Berlin, taking volunteers from General Police Duties (GPD). The task from then on was to be formally known as Close Protection (CP), but the responsibility would only be transferred from SIB to GPD personnel when suitable personnel had been specially trained.

As no formal CP training existed within the RMP, it was necessary to identify the training needs of such an undertaking and it was decided that an Officer and a SNCO would attend the VIP Protection Instructors Course delivered by 22 SAS. Captain Julian Backler RMP, who was then appointed Staff Captain to Lt Col Stock and SSgt John Redman, 19 (Sp) Pl Commander, were selected and in October 1974 attended the course.

Vehicle anti-ambush training on the first CP Course conducted at RTW, Werl.

Following their return to Germany, in 1975 (considerably fitter than they were when they left), Lt Col Stock ordered Maj Nick Crew, OC[2], 115 Pro Coy RMP to conduct a CP pilot course at Werl and together with Capt Backler, WO1 'Chic' Harding, SSgt Redman, SSgt John Knock, (who was now serving with 115 Pro Coy RMP), SSgt Dave Harding, Sgt Euan Grant and Cpl George Gilroy and an acquired copy of the US Secret Service Close Protection Training Manual, he established the Regimental Training Wing (RTW) and the first RMP Close Protection Course was conducted. It lasted three weeks and was designed to train Officers and JNCOs, who would then form a CP pool within BAOR. The finale of the course was an exercise with the DAPM, Maj Colin Watkins providing both the VIPs and enemy made up of brilliant young G2 Intelligence officers, known as the Wamel Liberation Front, (WLF), who lived in hirings in a village of the same name near the Möhne Dam. During training, improvisation played an important part and it was during one of the exercises that the VIP, Maj Gen Peter Walsh DSO GOC, 3 Armd Div, in an act of daring-do, escaped in a rowing boat across the reservoir. In these early days, resources were hard to come by and even the visiting RAF APM attended some training using his own BMC1800 staff car. Sadly, this resulted in its losing a door; thankfully, it was the APM driving at the time!

1975 saw the end of close protection as a SIB responsibility and, in 1976, Maj Crew and his team of instructors co-ordinated an 'official' BG course that

---

2   Maj Crew has been cited as being an 'ebullient and brilliant officer'. He retired from the army quite early and set up Winguard International. However, he sadly died whilst in his early 40s.

Maj Pete Townsend (in cap) as part of the protection team for Her Majesty Queen Elizabeth II whilst visiting Germany in 1977

Close protection isn't all about fast cars and helicopters!

took place in Bulford on the outskirts of Salisbury Plain.

RTW was not formally established with a Unit Identification Number (UIN) or Equipment Table causing no end of problems when muddling through the staff work required to co-ordinate such an organisation. However, 3.3 Litre Vauxhall Ventura cars and drivers were provided by 19 (Sp) Pl, (formerly Special Patrol Group RMP), 101 Pro Coy RMP based in Monchengladbach (before moving to Rheindahlen) and incorporated into the expanding pool of CP operatives. Because of the valuable experience gained whilst dealing with the Soviet Mission (SOXMIS)[3] in BAOR, overtly supporting covert anti-surveillance operations, carried out by 28 Sect (Int) and surge ops, when local RMP units required support with their policing operations, members of the platoon were seen as a valuable asset to the new arena of CP. Volunteers for the CP course were also sourced from 247 (Berlin) Pro Coy RMP and BAOR NCOs were sent to reinforce the Berlin-based CP NCOs when required.

Although the platoon never gained a UIN, under the command of Maj Peter Townsend it operated in an ad-hoc kind of way, putting together teams as were required when HQ BAOR deemed the threat upon a visiting dignitary warranted protection. This included Her Majesty The Queen, in the summer of 1977, when she visited units in BAOR to mark her Silver Jubilee, for which Maj Townsend was appointed MBE for his planning and execution of the detailed escort programme. RTW also managed to send a further two operators to Hereford to attend the CP Instructor Course, Major Tony Waygood and Chic Harding and when they returned the foundations of the Close Protection Team (BAOR) were laid.

On a weekend in 1978, information found its way to the media that the Deputy Supreme Allied Commander Europe (DSACEUR) was to be next General Officer Commanding of Northern Ireland and, given the situation and nature of the appointment, a CP team drawn from various units within BAOR was quickly deployed to SHAPE. On the Monday, the DAPM, Major Watkins, and his Chief Clerk SSgt Bill Sheridan BEM travelled to SHAPE to formally establish the team and operation producing Standard Operational Procedures (SOPs) on the spot. After three days, the team were left to carry on the mission with Maj Watkins and SSgt Sheridan returning to HQ 3 Armd Bde in Soest,

---

3 SOXMIS Soviet Military Mission. This was a small group of Soviet military observers, that operated in each of the Allied sectors of West Germany throughout the Cold War. Members of 19 (Sp) Pl supported the mission to counter this 'threat' and were known as 'white mice', due to the white 2.8 litre Ford Granada cars they drove, which were used to block in SOXMIS vehicles when the soviets were in places they should not have been.

The visit of H.R.H Princess Anne to Lübbecke, 1984.

where the DAPM was instructed to formally establish a Germany-based CP team and subsequently CP Team Germany (CP (G)) was born.

CP training in Germany continued at RTW, Werl until 1979/80, when all RMP CP training was centralised at 'Block 30' at the training area at Longmoor, Hampshire. In 1984, HRH Princess Anne visited Lübbecke, near Minden in Germany. During her time there, she was afforded close protection by Maj Nick Crew, who can be seen in the following photograph wearing a dark suit just behind the princess. The blonde lady in a suit to the left of shot is a German Police Personal Protection Officer (PPO).

Throughout the nineteen eighties the RMP, including Sgt 'Fritz' Farenholz and Cpl 'Paddy' McMichael, continued to support visiting VIPs, including Prime Minister Margaret Thatcher and the late Lord Younger, the Conservative Defence Minister. With the end of the Cold War in 1991, 19 (Sp) Pl disbanded. However, with the continued threat from Irish dissidents operating in BAOR, CPT (G) continued to provide close protection to visiting VIPs until 2007, when it moved to Longmoor and eventually became a mission of requirement rather than a standing team.

The Princess Royal was the victim of a kidnap attempt on 20th March

Sgt 'Woody' Woodward RMP can be seen providing protection to Princess Anne whilst visiting troops in Germany in 20 which had taken over the responsibility of Close Protection in Germany following the closure of CPT (G) in 2007.

1974. The Princess was travelling back to Buckingham Palace with her husband Capt Mark Phillips following a charity event when her limousine was forced to stop by a Ford Escort driven by Ian Ball. Ball then fired shots at the royal party wounding her Special Branch bodyguard, her chauffeur and a member of the press. Ball was tackled by a passerby and arrested by a police officer, who arrived at the scene. Ian Ball told Princess Anne that he intended to kidnap her and give the £3million ransom money to the NHS.

On Fri 29 Jul 11, at 1200 hrs, His Royal Highness Prince Philip, Duke of Edinburgh flew into Paderborn Airport where 3 members of CPU, RMP met him on the tarmac in order to provide Close Protection during his visit to the Queen's Royal Hussars at Athlone Barracks, in his capacity as Colonel-in-Chief of the regiment. CPU provided two Range Rovers for the tasking, which were driven from Longmoor in the UK.. The visit passed without incident and, prior to his departure, Prince Philip was kind enough to pose for a rare photograph with the team.

Chapter 4

Early Training in the UK and 'Block 30'

CP continued to evolve in BAOR until 1976 when it became apparent that demand for RMP Close Protection support was becoming more demanding and a focal point was required closer to home. Subsequently, it was decided CP training and operations should move to the UK. Meanwhile, Cpls Dave Harding and Pete Glover were serving together at the Advanced Training Wing at the RMPTC Chichester and were joined by Sgts John Knock and Hughie Grant. As all had Close Protection experience and a keen ability to instruct they were requested to devise a programme for a CP training course specific to the role of the RMP; as the SAS way of doing business was not conducive to the image of the RMP. Cpl Glover was responsible for teaching 'Booby Trap and Explosive Recognition' and by his own admission took much pleasure in setting ambushes and scaring the students … realistic training! After much planning, the first 'new generation' CP course was conducted in Tidworth in 1976, was critically assessed by members of 22 SAS and was, of course, visited by numerous 'bigwigs'. Although CP courses had been conducted before, it is fair to say that these four NCOs laid the foundation for what was to follow and remains largely extant today.

In late 1979, Capt Fred Boothby along with SSgts John Knock, Dave Harding, Chic Harding and Sgt Grant were tasked to find a suitable location for RMP CP training. They liaised with the Commandant of Longmoor Training Camp and Block 30, a 2nd World War Nissan Hut, was offered as a training and administrative office. The scoping team also accepted a large house that had been the Garrison Commander's residence and is still under the control of RMP CP.

Following his posting to PM (A) as Deputy Assistant Adjutant General (DAAG), Nick Crew contrived to get Colin Watkins posted to Longmoor as the first OC of the Close Protection Training Wing (CPTW). Among his staff were those who had attended the SAS CP module and, seemingly synonymous with RMP CP up until then, SSgt John Knock, (CSM), SSgt Euan Grant and

Walking drills on the Urban Training Complex Longmoor 1978.

Ladysmith House 1982: Royal Military Police Close Protection Course 1982
Rear Row: Sgt George McDonald, Cpl Fritz Farenholz, Cpl Roy
Swales, US MP, 2, 3, 4, 5, 6, US MP, Cpl Dick Jones, 7
Front Row: Capt Colin Findlay, 8, 9, Sgt Mick Bottomley, WO1 UE Grant, Maj
Ken Greenland, SSgt Alan Cray, 10, Capt Ian Prosser, Fl Lt Mike Brzinski RAF

EARLY TRAINING IN THE UK AND 'BLOCK 30'   93

FCO Drivers' Course 1978 with Instructors Ken Blake (front left), Colin Watkins (rear left), Alan Cray (rear) and Euan Grant (front right) (the lady is a representative from the FCO whose name is unknown)

Sgt Steve Hardacre (PT and CP Drills), Sgt Alan Cray (Weapons, Explosives and Search) and SSgt Ken Blake,(CP Drills and Counter Terrorism), SSgt Blake, who had spent 9 months with the German Counter Terrorist Unit, Einsatzkommando 3 in Berlin, and Cpl Alan Hilliam, who was the 'Q' and ensured all kit and equipment necessary to carry out the relevant tasks were readily available and, finally, the 'wing' clerk, Cpl Ross Greenwood.

For administration and overall senior command the CP Training Wing came under the Commandant Royal Military Police Training Centre (RMPTC) at Chichester.

Once in place, the 'Wing' provided CP courses of 6 weeks duration for 24 students. Initially, all students were RMP but later personnel from the RN Regulators, RM Police, RAFP and, on occasions, UK civil and foreign military police officers even Lt Col Mike Ramsey (later PM (BAOR) attended the course and passed with flying colours, which was a considerable feat for a senior officer in his forties. During those early years, the team conducted nine courses with anywhere between 18-24 NCOs, which led to about 200 trained CP personnel, allowing for an approximate 60% pass rate.

In order to attend the CP course, RMP volunteers were required to attend a pre-selection board to assess their fitness, skill-at-arms and, above all else, their steadfastness and suitability for deployment as bodyguards. The boards were held in every theatre at six monthly intervals.

The course content was very similar to that of today; weapon training, passive anti-surveillance training, vehicle and building search, reaction to attack and tactical driving. In addition to the 'Wing' instructors, specialists from the Royal Engineer Search Wing, the Royal Army Ordnance Corps, Explosive Ordnance Disposal and the Intelligence Corps Centre also provided their expertise. To ensure the students had fully grasped all that had been taught the training culminated in a final exercise, named Ex WORKING DAY, and was conducted much as Ex WATCHTOWER is today (though on a slightly smaller scale). The enemy was usually provided by 21 SAS, who had a habit of driving their vehicle through the front door of Ladysmith House to affect an attack. Col Martin Burton (late Royal Army Education Corps) played the role of 'Marco Brutoni', a vital witness who was going to testify against the Mafia! There may have been a problem with the Mafia in the 80s but nowadays the scenarios are more in tune with current operations.

During the exercise phase, the students are constantly watched and on one occasion they had gone to the launderette in Liphook, a local village, where they openly talked about the course and the exercise. Un-noticed by the students was a modest looking Indian couple doing their laundry. Following the exercise debrief by the 'enemy' the Indian man, an SAS trooper, who had been in the launderette with his wife, stood up and much to their embarrassment identified the students. Although he didn't say so, the message was clear – 'Talking in public is dangerous' and was reminiscent of the messages of World War II such as 'Loose Lips Sinks Ships' etc.

The course ended with a comprehensive debrief and students were quickly informed of their results. At this stage most would pass, as, by this point, those who could not keep up with the pace of training, or were found not suitable, had already been returned to their units.

In addition to the CP course, training was established for both military and Foreign Office VIP drivers, which eventually became known as the Protective Mobile Skills (PMS) Course and then the Close Protection Tactical Driving Course. Students continue to come from countries all over the world including Burma, Iran, Israel, Pakistan and Sudan and are being taught how to drive defensively when with a VIP. Training then continued at Block 30 until 2000 when the wheels of change bought about the CPU.

Chapter 5

Supporting the Foreign and Commonwealth Office (FCO)

Since the 1950s, RMP had been involved in formulated escorts of some description operating from London District Pro Coy (LONDIST), at that time located within Kensington Palace (before moving to Rochester Row). Armed with .38 revolvers concealed under heavy duty motorcycle top coats, riding either a BSA M20 or Triumph 500 V twins, Cpl (later WO1) Tony Johnson was one of a number of NCOs, who had the task of escorting a government car, which would be carrying the civilian employee wages (then paid in cash) from Whitehall to Army units in London, principally the REME Workshops at Bittacy Hill in Millhill. The escort was very low key and was most likely in place to deter the IRA. Operations continued from within LONDIST RMP NCOs and evolved into the escorting of parliamentary figures including the Prime Minister and Foreign Secretary on a regular basis in order to protect locations and the government 'red boxes'.[1] Cpl Johnson assisted Special Branch in 1964 and 1965 respectively when he escorted the Prime Minister Harold Wilson and Foreign Secretary, Patrick Gordon Walker, to Rhodesia. This relationship had been established by the OC London District, Maj Paul Williams and the FCO Protocol Department. Maj Williams later joined the FCO and, under the command of Maj Collin Watkins, the RMP saw themselves heavily involved in special duties such as the Queen's Birthday Parade and international conferences hosted by the Government in Lancaster House. Sgt 'Percy' Powell RMP had been at LONDIST since 1965 and been actively involved in escort duties from LONDIST including the provision of protection for Lord George Brown MP, Deputy Leader of the Labour Party when he visited Paris and Strasburg. For these trips, Sgt Powell was restricted to hotel security and safeguarding the Diplomatic boxes but in 1967 things got far more interesting.

---

1   The term "Red Box" informally refers to a ministerial box used by ministers in the British government to carry their documents. Similar in appearance to a briefcase, they are primarily used to hold and transport official departmental papers from place to place.

96 DETER SUPPRESS EXTRACT!

From left: Sgt Percy Powell RMP, UK Gurkha soldier,
Cpl 'Fletch' Fletcher and Cpl Jack Lavelle

By 1967, the Vietnam War was into its 11th year and one afternoon in June, whilst sitting in an office in London, Sgt Powell received a telephone call from the Provost Marshall's office offering him a post seconded to the British Embassy in Saigon. Following increased attacks on Western properties in Saigon, since 1966 a Sergeant and two RMP Corporals from 200 Provost Company in Singapore had been sent to the Embassy on three month rotational attachments and along with a detachment of Gurkha soldiers, they were responsible for the security of the Embassy, the Ambassador, Sir Crawford Murray MacLehose, and employees. Following a three-month Vietnamese language course, one on one language tuition paid for by the FCO and reel to reel language tapes, in October Sgt Powell boarded a New Zealand Airforce Bristol Freighter and flew into Saigon. After taking over from Sgt Colin Lumi RMP, Sgt Powell joined Cpl Fred Fletcher RMP and Cpl Jack Lavelle RMP from Singapore and took over responsibility for the team. Sgt Powell's appointment was different from that of his predecessors in that he was attached to the Embassy as a member of

SUPPORTING THE FCO 97

Photograph taken by Sgt Powell with the graveyard wall beyond.

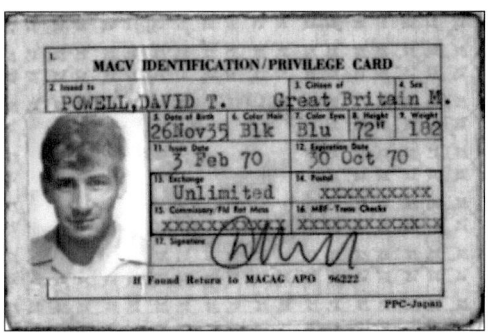

the Diplomatic Staff on a 12 month posting reporting directly to the Deputy Head of Mission and, completely outside a military chain of command, he didn't even have rules for opening fire. Living to the North East of the city, both the Embassy and the Corporal's accommodation were some way away to the South West with the Corporal's house being located next to the South Vietnamese Forces Headquarters.

Sgt Powell's house overlooked a graveyard and he observed an unusually

Above: Photograph taken by Sgt Powell whilst enjoying a helicopter flight with SM Holt showing a US riverine patrol along the coast.

Sergeant Major Class 2 Holt USMP with Sgt Percy Powell RMP outside the US provost Marshall's office, Long Binh Post, about 15 miles outside Saigon.

SUPPORTING THE FCO

Sgt Powell at the gates of the British Embassy in Saigon.

high number of funerals taking place but at the time thought little of it. The reasons for these were to become apparent later.

Back in the UK, PM(A) was Brig Dickie Richards, (who in 1959/60 commanded LONDIST), and was a firm friend of the 18th MP Bde Comd. Brigadier General Karl W Gustafeson. PM(A) 'introduced his boys' to the US Provost Marshall's office and a liaison was quickly appointed. Sergeant Major Class 2 Holt was charged with taking his British colleagues under his wing and as the relationship between the two allies grew, Sgt Powell and the team were very well looked after.

Sgt Powell was very fortunate also to forge sound relationships with the US 5th Special Forces Group, 8000 green berets commanded by Col Mike Healy. Following the events of the Chinese New Year, they provided a great deal of support, in particular Sgt First Class Dick Fowler and Sgt First Class 'Doc' Spivey, both of whom had a logistics background and adopted Sgt Powell and his team.

In order for Sgt Powell to pass freely through the city, he was issued a number of passes, a Vietnamese ID Card, an Embassy pass and a pass from the Ministry of Foreign Affairs.

The Chinese New Year was on the 29th January 1968 and was the Year of the Monkey. There had been a long- standing agreement between the US and

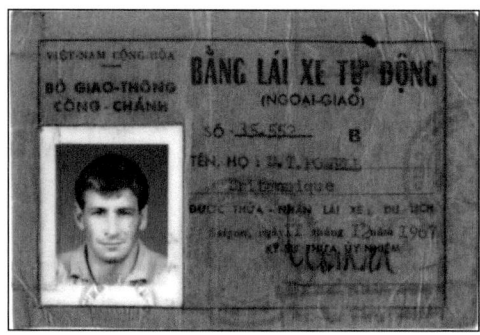
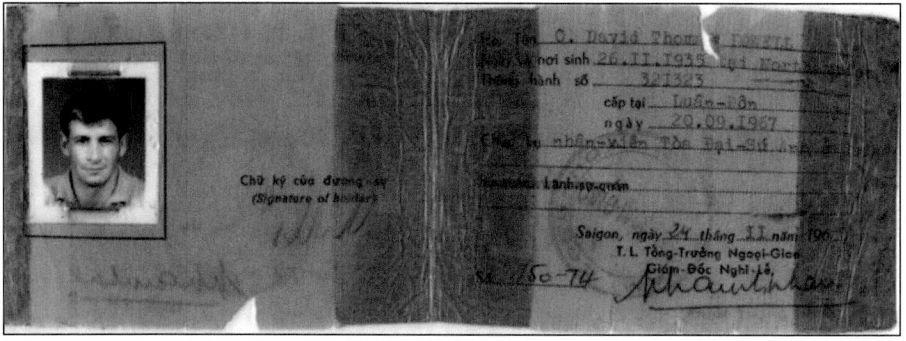
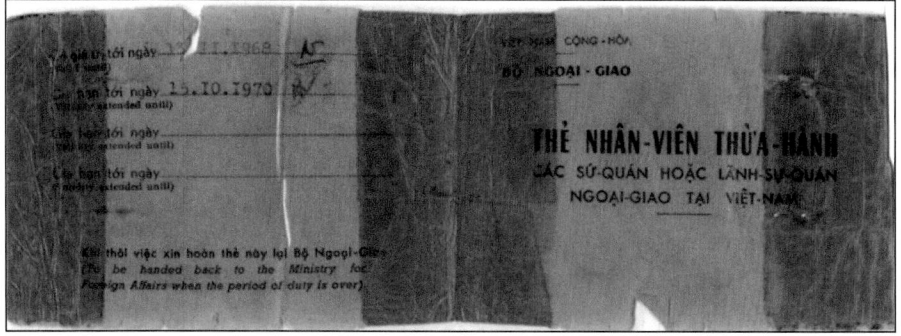

Map of Saigon carried by Sgt Powell.

allies, South Vietnamese Forces, North Vietnamese Forces and Viet Cong that hostilities would cease for the New Year celebrations and instead would be a declared holiday. With soldiers withdrawn from their posts to allow them to celebrate, the Tet Offensive began and attacks key towns and installations all over Vietnam by the Viet Cong began, Saigon included. Sgt Powell recalls the events of that evening:

> Firecrackers went off and tracer rounds were being fired into the sky for most of the night. It wasn't until about 6 o'clock the following morning my servant told me that the Viet Cong were attacking Saigon and other towns. Local TV and radio had been cut off so, switching to the US Army radio channel, it was reported that fighting had been witnessed at a number of key locations including the airport and the Presidential Palace. By 8 o'clock I had made the decision to head across town and to check on Fred and Jack, who lived next door to the South Vietnamese Forces HQ and a prime target, and make sure the Embassy was still secure and the Gurkha guard force was safe. Dressed in civvies not uniform, (I didn't want to get lifted!), and in

From left: Sgt Percy Powell, Sgt First Class 'Doc' Spivey and Sgt First Class Dick Fowler
Rear: Cpl 'Fletch' Fletcher

The US Embassy as seen from the British Embassy. The damage from the rocket attack can be seen clearly.

possession of my Embassy ID card, I grabbed my bicycle and headed off in the right direction. The bike allowed me to dart in and out and was very low profile. Coming to a major intersection, the airport being right, town left, there were about 10 local policemen lying in the prone position firing their M2 carbines up the street in the direction of the airport. In Vietnamese, I shouted for them to cease fire so that I could cross. They held their fire and as I crossed on my bicycle I could see skirmishes about 200 yards way.

Travelling further into town towards the Presidential Palace, there was fierce fighting taking place with helicopter gunships firing machine guns and jets from the South Vietnamese Airforce firing rockets at the Viet Cong. Parking my bike I watched, transfixed. With a grandstand view, it was like watching a film. I had to break away and get the Corporals, but with all major routes closed off, it was a case of putting my bike on my shoulder and, using back gardens, I made my way. With the sounds of fighting at the HQ close by, I arrived at Fred and Jack's house. They were ok … but had no bread for breakfast. Back on my bike, I pedalled away from the fighting to the bakers which, unsurprisingly, was closed. Smelling fresh bread in the air, I banged on the door and convinced the baker to sell me some bread. It was on route back, the mortar landed. Feeling the shockwave I took to the back gardens again and was soon back at the house. That afternoon, two US Special Forces Sergeants, who we had befriended, arrived with boxes of M16 rifles, clips and grenades, we exchanged our usual pleasantries (but no signatures!) and they left. We stayed put until the following day when we were able to visit the Embassy. Thankfully it was intact. However, the Viet Cong had taken up a position on the pavement in front of our front gates and engaged the US Embassy over the street with RPG, causing minor damage. The fighting had subsided significantly and together with Maj Bedford Russell, a British Officer form the Intelligence and Security Corps, we headed into town for a recce. Marshall Law had been imposed. However, being in uniform, we had free run of the city. We found evidence of the fighting and dead Viet Cong (the bodies were left on the street for some time as a message to others) but apart from that the city was very quiet. With no rules of engagement and a Wild West feel to the place we were very thankful there was no one around. After taking a few photos, we returned to the Embassy. The Embassy didn't open for a few days and it wasn't long before I was requested to drive the Ambassador in his Austin Princess to a meeting with the US Ambassador to South Vietnam, Ellsworth F. Bunker and it took over a month for life to

Following the fighting Sgt Powell (closest to camera) and Maj Russell ventured out onto the streets. Behind Sgt Powell are the bodies of two Viet Cong fighters who had been travelling in the white truck.

The same white truck. The damage caused by gunfire can be seen clearly.

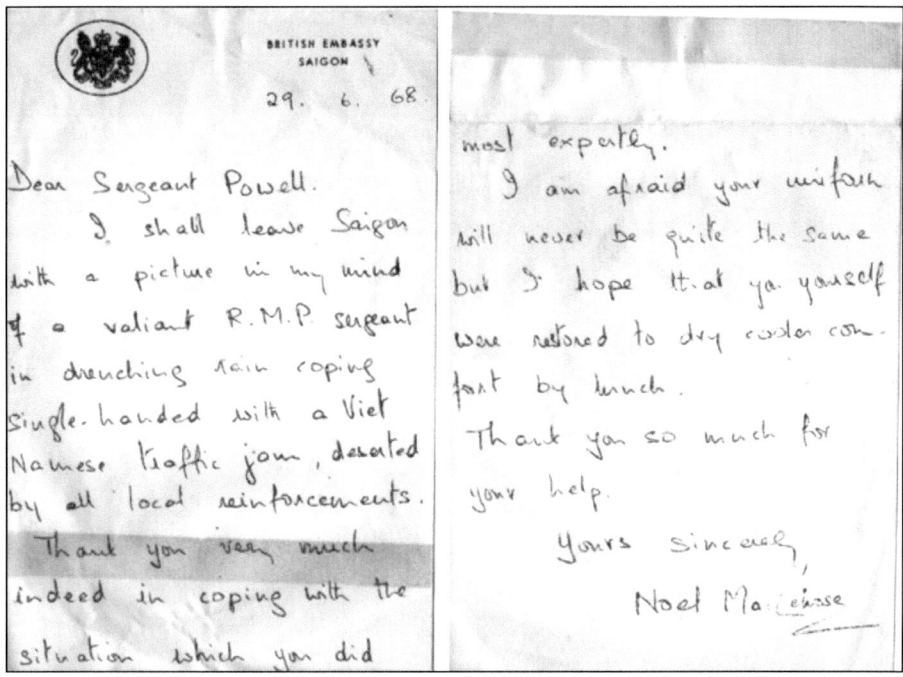

Letter of thanks to Sgt Powell written by the Ambassador's wife, Noel.

return to normal.

And what of the funerals taking place opposite Sgt Powell's house? They were staged by the Viet Cong, who were burying weapons and ammunition in preparation for the offensive.

When the US Ambassador moved around the city in his motorcade, it created a mass of traffic problems. On one afternoon, Sgt Powell was dressed in his best uniform with all his leatherwork freshly whitened, and a typhoon described as a solid wall of water had just arrived. The US Ambassador and his vehicular entourage was creating carnage in the streets. The British Ambassador and his wife needed to attend an appointment so, jumping out of the car, Sgt Powell directed traffic and got things moving. His uniform ruined, he got back in the car and they continued on their way. Thinking nothing more of it, Sgt Powell received a letter of thanks from the Ambassador's wife, Noel.

On completion of his attachment, Sgt Powell was posted to Singapore but returned to Saigon in October 1969 for a further 12 months.

In 1981 Cpl (later WO2) Andy Mudd was posted to London District Provost Company and, having completed the CP Course the year before whilst with 227 Pro Coy, was heavily involved in the escorts and remembers 'stagging on' with Cpl Mal Davies outside of Margaret Thatcher's hotel room in Brussels armed with a revolver borrowed from one of her own Special Branch protection team. The RMP were able to provide Low Risk Search Teams, trained by the Royal Engineer Search Wing, and two RMP Search Dog Handlers. The NCOs would be armed at such conferences and, in order to be compliant with civil police firearms legislation, several RMP personnel including WO2 Mick Cross and Cpl Ken Blake, attended firearms training with Metropolitan Police Firearms unit known as D11.[2]

The SAS were first deployed as bodyguards in 1966 and in 1972 the Parliamentary Under Secretary in the FCO, Sir Anthony Royle requested an SAS bodyguard accompany him to South Africa instead of a Special Branch officer. This gave the SAS a foot in the FCO door and a Close Protection Cell was formed within the Counter Revolutionary Warfare Wing at Hereford that saw specific 'bodyguard' training. The first Principals were not British diplomats but foreign heads of state, who it was felt had important good will to offer the UK, and also sensitive Warsaw Pact defectors, who had ended up in Great Britain.

In 1975, the FCO employed a civilian security firm called Keeni Meani services (KMS), which comprised mainly ex SAS personnel, who were to protect at-risk Ambassadors and Embassy staff. KMS continued to provide protection until 1978, when questions were raised in Parliament as to the legal status of KMS employees. If they ever drew their weapons in anger whilst protecting a principal abroad, would they be given full diplomatic immunity and what would be the effect upon the government at home? KMS were, after all, a private security firm with each bodyguard earning £20,000, (about £80,000 today) of taxpayer's money.

With the election of Mrs Thatcher's administration in 1979 and following the assassination of Airy Neave MP a month before, it was decided that it was no longer suitable to leave the protection of diplomats in the hands of a civilian security firm, regardless of their experience.

By 1979, the RMP were well established in the role of providing CP in

---

2   The Firearms Wing, as it was originally named, was formed as part of the Civil Defence and Communications Branch or D6 by its designation in response to the murder of three police officers by Harry Roberts in 1966 in what became known as 'The Shepherd's Bush Murders' or 'Massacre of Braybrook Street'. D6 was later renamed D11and, following a number of different designations, became the Central Operations Specialist Firearms Command (CO19) as it is known today. CO19 and CPU still enjoy a close relationship.

SUPPORTING THE FCO 107

Front cover of the Executive Committee of the Army Board document (now declassified) confirming that the responsibility of Close Protection within the army would fall upon the Royal Military Police.

operational theatres. This, together with their long-standing escort capability in peace and war all over the world, resulted in the RMP being the logical, ideal choice to take over from KMS. In 1981, the RMP deployed its first teams into Uganda and the Lebanon. In 1982, the Argentines invaded the Falkland Islands and it was realised by the FCO that its Embassies in South America, especially Uruguay were at risk. Subsequently, the FCO requested the RMP send a team out to Montevideo; However, due to the Falklands campaign being the biggest military campaign since the Suez crises in 1966, the RMP could not meet the request. Subsequently, KMS had its swan song providing the team required in South America. The RMP soon asserted itself and sent

Maj Colin Watkins in Abey, the British Ambassador's summer house in the mountains outside Beirut.

a training/advisory team consisting of two Warrant Officers, including Alan Cray, to South America in the early 1980s.

Following an Executive Committee Army Board (ECAB) decision on 13th February 1980, (between CP Course 4 and 5), the RMP became the operational leader in CP within the military and evolved along two different paths, continuing the provision of CP to military commanders and providing CP in support of the Foreign and Commonwealth Office. During the transition, KMS were highly professional and did everything they could to ensure a smooth handover to the RMP. At the request of the civilian police, assistance could also be given to them and in 1980, King Hussein visited an air show in Middle Wallop and, although security cordons were placed up to three miles away, it was a RMP CP team which worked alongside the King's own CP team ensuring his safety.

Maj Watkins, as OC CP Wing, with support and direction given by Col Peter Durrant and Col Mike Deans at HQ PM (Army), harnessed and nurtured the relationship between the RMP and the FCO and undertook all operational liaison with Chief Superintendent Harry Nichols Metropolitan Police Special Branch Officer and FCO Security Officer.

SUPPORTING THE FCO

WO1 (RSM) John O'Donnell lowering the flag at the British High Commission in Rhodesia.

As a result of the civil war in Lebanon and unrest in Uganda in 1981, authority was given by PM(A) and the MOD for two teams to deploy in support of the FCO with a mandate to provide protection to the respective Ambassadors, taking the reins from KMS. Maj Watkins and Ch. Supt Nichols flew to both countries and, whilst staying with the respective Ambassador and High Commissioner, liaised with the ex-SAS commercial security officers and made an operational assessment of the situation on the ground.

On returning to Longmoor, two teams, each comprising of 5 NCOs, were to be deployed and two briefing rooms were set up for each post and advanced, specific training was delivered, the first CP Pre Deployment Training (PDT). The Kampala Team was led by Sgt Bob Giles deployed in November 1981 and the Beirut team by SSgt Ken Blake in December 1981. Both teams were briefed in detail on their particular locations by various experts from both the MOD and the FCO. Just prior to deployment, both teams were visited by the Director of Military Operations (DMO) and the Chief of the General Staff, Gen (later Field Marshal) Sir Edwin Bramall KG, GCB, OBE, MC, DL, JP.

In 1980, John O'Donnell was Regimental Sergeant Major (RSM) of LONDIST and was heavily involved in diplomatic escort duties for the likes of Margaret Thatcher and other parliamentarians. It was as a result of these duties he was approached by the FCO with a view of taking a CP team to Rhodesia to provide protection to Lord Soames, who was at that time the Interim Governor of the British Colony of Southern Rhodesia. As a result of the Lancaster House Agreement, Rhodesia had gained independence from Great Britain and times were turbulent. The FCO bought new uniforms (not yet issued to serving troops) and weapons for the new team and it wasn't long before the RSM and his team were an important part of the mission in Rhodesia. At the time there was a British Monitoring Force in place led by Lt Col Parker Bowles. On the 18th April 1980, the RSM was recognised for the professional manner in which his team had conducted themselves whilst providing protection for Lord Soames and his wife and was invited to lower the Union Jack in a ceremony that marked the end of Colonial rule in Rhodesia. The flag lowering ceremony took place with an audience that included Prince Charles and Lord Soames. This saw the end of Rhodesia and the birth of Zimbabwe.

The Provost Marshal (Army) of the time declared that 'the lads had to become social chameleons' (which is still the case today) and the following account by SSgt Ken Blake gives an insight into how the relationship between the RMP and the FCO became what it is today.

> The Lebanon in 1981 had not resolved the issues that had brought it to civil war in 1975. Various groupings of either Christian or Muslim militias were operating on the ground and there was fighting, not only between the Christians and the Muslims, but also between various Muslim groups. West Beirut was divided into what is best described as 'tribal areas' with a mass of checkpoints manned by various militias, the PLO and the Arab Defence force (mainly Syrian soldiers, who had been deployed to the country following the civil war). Anti-aircraft positions were dug in around various buildings and Toyota jeeps with machine guns mounted patrolled the streets. The inhabitants of West Beirut, and visitors (from east Beirut) were often subjected to intimidation at these checkpoints and indeed some militias were particularly known for their desire to rob and murder victims. The most dangerous time for all inhabitants was when Israeli air force planes flew overhead. This was not because they dropped bombs but because of the amount of anti-aircraft munitions and gunfire that was sent into the air by the militias on the ground. It literally rained lead on such occasions.
>
> East Beirut was controlled by the Christian Militia, which was led by Bashir Geymel, whose brother, Pierre, would eventually be elected president of Lebanon and thereafter assassinated. East Beirut was relatively calm and

law-abiding. The only difficulty was moving between the two parts of the city. The centre had been heavily shelled and fought over in the civil war and snipers still operated amongst the debris. The two main crossing points were through the port and within the city through a checkpoint known as the 'Museum Crossing'. Travel throughout the rest of the country could be hazardous depending on whose area you were travelling through and any local fighting militias.

The British Embassy and all UK staff were based in West Beirut with the Embassy building situated on the Corniche, a sea-front location, about half a mile from the American Embassy. The RMP CP team, comprising of 5 NCOs, arrived on the 18th December and were accommodated in a flat behind the Riviera Hotel on the Corniche, a short walk from the Embassy. The team spent two weeks taking over from the KMS personnel. The team, although experienced in operations in Northern Ireland, had never served before in such hostile surroundings. It was also a matter of being fully responsible for their own domestic arrangements-shopping and cooking their own meals, laundry and cleaning. Once fully operational, the team initially relied heavily upon the Ambassador's driver, Mohamed Itani BEM, for his local contacts and knowledge. Duties comprised providing the Ambassador with a personal bodyguard and Personal Escort Section (PES). In addition, 2 NCOs were required to control access to the Embassy during opening hours. At the end of the working day, the personal Bodyguard [BG] and 2 members of the PES remained within the Ambassador's residence.

In mid January 1982, the team was reinforced by a further 3 NCOs following intelligence reports that the British Ambassador was being targeted by a Shiite Militia with close links to the Syrian authorities. During the early days, the team all formed the opinion that the diplomats and employees were either shell-shocked or had become slightly insane within their surroundings. It became apparent as time went on that you get used to your surroundings and, like the aforementioned, we, the team, no longer flinched or looked for cover when gunfire and anti-aircraft fire were occurring – it became just part of your daily routine and you just carried on as normal.

The months preceding June were busy but fortunately no attack was ever mounted against the Ambassador. However, members of staff were targeted and intimidated. The team was called upon to protect a locally-employed member of staff, a Sunni Muslim, who had been kidnapped and then released by Shiite group, until he was flown back to the UK. During this period, the

French diplomats suffered extremely badly with attacks being mounted upon them both whilst mobile and in their residences. In May 2002, the British Embassy reduced its number of UK-based staff to minimum levels in order to reduce risk. By this stage, the team had established excellent relations with the American, German and in particular the French close protection teams.

The team deployed with 9mm pistols and sub-machine guns. A surprise arrival from the UK courtesy of the RAF, were nine Heckler Koch HK53 weapons. We removed the packaging to discover them still covered in grease. Having cleaned them, read the manuals and worked out how they operated we got the Ambassador to agree to let us fire them in the basement of the Embassy in a makeshift range. They fired, hit the target and seemed to work ok – we never had cause to fire them in anger for the rest of our tour.

When the Ambassador was out of the country on leave or business, the team would look after the Counselor, who was the No2 in the Embassy. It was on one of those occasions, whilst residing in the flat of the Counselor in a building next door to the Embassy, that one of the team received a bullet wound to the foot. He had not been targeted but had simply had the misfortune to be standing on the balcony whilst a wedding was taking place some two kilometres away. It was the custom when attending a wedding to fire your weapon into the air – unfortunately, what is fired up must come down and in this case an AK47 round entered his right foot.

Team members managed to get at least two weeks R & R during their 12 month tour of duty flying in and out of Beirut airport. Sadly, when it came to the Team Leader taking his R & R in August the airport was closed and therefore he departed and returned from R & R by means of a small pleasure vessel via Cyprus – not exactly business class!

On the 6th June 1982 the Israeli Army entered the Lebanon and began its advance towards Beirut. We would move through their lines at weekends when travelling from Beirut to Abey, the mountain residence of the Ambassador. Life became tense in West Beirut as the Israelis advanced. Israeli naval vessels would patrol offshore and on occasion fire shells into the city and attacks from the air became more prevalent. On one occasion the shells from the Israeli warships were passing directly over the residence and landing about one to two kilometres away. The Ambassador was taking an afternoon nap on his bed and when asked by the Team Leader to descend into the cellar for safety – he refused. The Team Leader sat on the end of the bed. When asked what he was doing he informed the Ambassador that

HM The Queen with PM(A) Brig Mike Mathews on her left during her visit to the Royal Military Police Training Centre, Chichester as Colonel-in Chief of the RMP in 1977, the Silver Jubilee year (Cpl Glover can be seen to the left sporting a 'Zapat' moustache).

On Fri 29 Jul 11, at 1200 hrs His Royal Highness Prince Phillip, Duke of Edinburgh flew into Paderborn Airport where 3 members of CPU, RMP met him on the tarmac in order to provide Close Protection during his visit to the Queen's Royal Hussars at Athlone Barracks, in his capacity as Colonel in Chief of the regiment. CPU provided two Range Rovers for the tasking which were driven from the UK from Longmoor. The visit passed without incident and prior to his departure, Prince Philip was kind enough to pose for a rare photograph with the team. His Royal Highness Prince Philip, Duke of Edinburgh and his RMP Close Protection Team. From Left: Sgt Barry Key, Cpl Steven Humphrey and Cpl Ben Mears.

Following the Ambassador's armoured Jaguar in Beirut in the 1980s.

Members of Close Protection teams have travelled around the world. This scene is north of Khartoum, Sudan, and was photographed by the author during his deployment there in 2007.

A CP Team training outside Ladysmith House getting ready for deployment to Kampala, 1989.

Sgt Mark Slater RMP with Cpl (later SSgt) 'Harry' Hodson
RMP with a Land Rover 110 in Kampala, 1988.

Sir Richard Branson (centre) with HMA François Gordon and the RMP CP Team including SSgt 'Wurze' Young at the rear (with moustache), 1997.

From the decision being made to having boots on the ground took the Haiti CP Team from Longmoor just 72 hours. From left: Cpl Ben Slater RMP, Cpl Ryan Banner RMP, SSgt Lloyd Paterson RMP, Capt Jim Devenney RMP, HMA Dom. Rep. Steve Fisher, Cpl Eddy Edmunds RMP, Sgt Dave Clarke RMP, Sgt 'Harry' Dearing RMP, Cpl 'Gaz' Irvin RMP, 2010.

Such is the reputation of RMP Close Protection teams, a story entitled 'Protection Squad' written by Mike Knowles with supporting artwork by Gordon Livingstone was published by Commando Comics in November 1993. The story followed the experiences of the fictional character LCpl Jack Johnson as he trained for and conducted Close Protection duties.

The synopsis of Commando 4245 *Protection Squad* read as follows:

Bored with paperwork and traffic duties, Lance-Corporal Jack Johnston of the Royal Military Police was on the lookout for excitement. So he volunteered for special duties and, after a spell of tough training, became a member of the elite Close Protection Squads. That was when he began to understand what real excitement was!

Story: Mike Knowles Cover Art: Ian Kennedy. Inside Art: Gordon Livingstone Commando © D.C. Thompson & Co. Ltd

An RMP CP operator in Baghdad with Lt Gen Rollo, 2008.

An RMP CP operator assigned to the Senior Civilian Representative in Afghanistan in 2010.

The author chatting with the Chief of the Defence Staff, Air Chief Marshal Sir 'Jock' Stirrup and Lt Gen Sir 'Rob' Fry RM, Senior British Representative in at LZ Washington within the 'Green Zone' Baghdad in 2006. Such are the circles in which RMP CP operators mix.

Ex Cpl James Crofts RMP (V) (left) and an RMP operator following one of many foot patrols with the Brigade Commander in Helmand Province, Afghanistan in 2010. The UGL can be seen fitted to Sgt Heron's C8 along with his wrist mounted GPS.

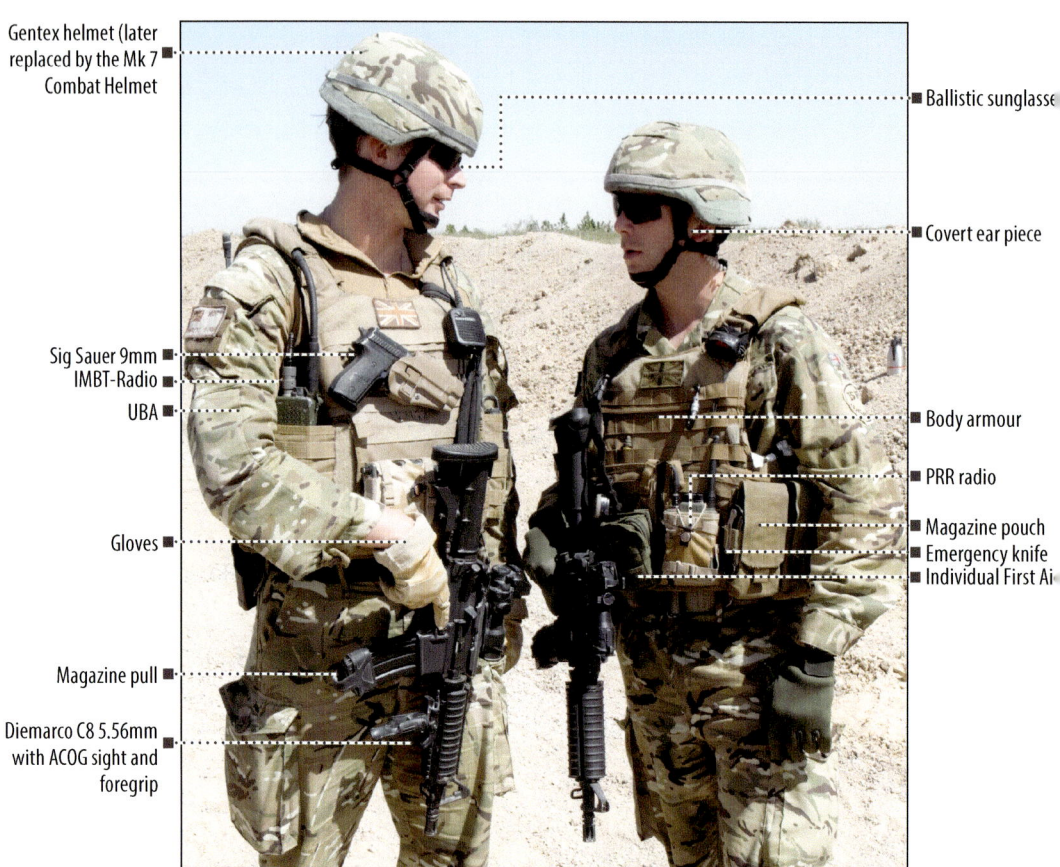

Kit and equipment of a CP Operator.

Capt Tony Cooper RMP in Afghanistan.

On patrol with American callsigns and Striker Armoured Personnel Carriers, north of Mosul, Iraq, 2006.

Cpl Mick Collier RMP (left) securing the ground prior to the arrival of the VIP somewhere in London. The photo was taken by a surveillance team, an excellent training recourse and teaching tool at CPU, 2010.

Without the help of agencies such as the civil police public roads could not be cut off to allow the Joint Forces Helicopter Support Unit to land a Lynx helicopter in order to extract the VIP group during Exercise Watchtower, 2010.

ROYAL MILITARY POLICE CLOSE PROTECTION TEAM (GERMANY)
CPL'S CHADDERTON, DAVIES, FOSTER, FENDLEY
SSGT McNEILL, CAPT TASKER, WO2 ROBERTS
1994

177 PROVOST COMPANY
1st REGIMENT
ROYAL MILITARY POLICE

BACK ROW: Cpl Atkinson IJ, Cpl Bolton SJ, Cpl Carswell P, Cpl Hopper JF, Cpl Bruning MA, Cpl Robson DC, Cpl Wilson IA, Cpl Hand DA, Cpl McCoubrey K, Cpl Williams RJ, Cpl Oldfield A.
CENTRE ROW: Cpl Mousley GntC, Cpl Lazard SGA, Cpl Harvey A, Cpl Shaw GT, Cpl Roberts M, Cpl Bartholomew NP, Cpl Bird MR, Cpl Gorton DR, Cpl Dredge PD, Cpl Johnson S, Cpl Dodds LJ

GOC (NI), COS (NI) COMMANDERS 39, 8 & 3 BRIGADE WITH 177 (SUPPORT) PLATOON

Thiepval Barracks, Lisburn, Northern Ireland.

November 1999

Back Row : Cpl Slater, Cpl Fairbrother, Cpl Burgess, Sgt Franklin RLC, Cpl Pullen, Cpl McGrath, Cpl Dutton, Cpl Jones, Cpl Keightley, Cpl Smith, Cpl Kelly, Cpl Whiteside.

Middle Row : LCpl Igo RLC, Cpl Stagg, Cpl Fowler, Cpl Littler, LCpl Toovey RLC, Cpl Mahon, Sgt Trowbridge, Sgt Martin, Cpl Thornley, LCpl Doughty RLC, Cpl Dodge, LCpl Board RLC, Cpl Mortimer, Cpl Robinson.

Front Row : SSgt Gibson, Capt PF Wellington, Brig PFO'RD Davidson-Houston OBE, Brig JNR Houghton OBE, Lt Gen Sir Hew Pike KCB DSO MBE, Brig JMJ Balfour OBE, Brig RM Brunt OBE, Lt Col JIS Plastow MBE, WO2 Newman, SSgt Haynes.

**HIGH REPRESENTATIVES CLOSE PROTECTION TEAM
SARAJEVO May – December 2003**

Mr Mirsad Tufo, Mr Dragan Grahovac, Cpl GN Wood, Cpl GA Statham, Cpl AJ Taylor, Cpl G Shankly, Mr Sead Palo.
Sgt CI Gibson, Sgt PW Lancaster, SSgt S Holland, Lord Ashdown, Lady Ashdown, Sgt PJ Shephard, Ian Patrick.

SENIOR CIVILIAN REPRESENTATIVE – AFGHANISTAN
CLOSE PROTECTION TEAM 01/10
APRIL 2010 – OCTOBER 2010

Cpl Mick Collier, LCpl Drew Bowness, Cpl 'Polly' Cairns, Cpl 'Mac' McLoughlin, Cpl Ben Bowsorth, 'Achilles' WO2 Richard Keightley, SCR Mark Sedwill, SSgt 'Royston' Vasey.

if he were to be blown up then the Team Leader would be the subject of a Court Martial – they would therefore 'endex' together if a shell fell short. The Ambassador agreed to move to the cellar!

West Beirut went into defensive mode and the occupants began to build blockades on the streets ready to defend themselves when the attack was mounted. West Beirut was eventually surrounded by Israeli Army and infantry attacks, supported by tanks and artillery fire, now added to the naval and air bombardment. A blackout was in place during the hours of darkness and movement after dark was fraught with dangers as trigger-happy occupants of checkpoints considered all movement other than theirs to be that of Israeli invaders! On one such dark night, the Ambassador required an urgent signal to be sent to London and two team members, who fortunately had the use of an armoured car, were dispatched to the Embassy from the residence. Engaged twice at two checkpoints by thankfully small arms fire they delivered the signal and made their way back to the residence. Only the port crossing point remained open and the following morning the Ambassador decided to evacuate to east Beirut. Led by the Ambassador's car a small convoy of British diplomats made their way across to East Beirut. It was a strange feeling – on the one hand of relief that we were getting the Ambassador, his wife and the remaining diplomats out of harm's way, but on the other hand a feeling of sadness at leaving the Lebanese people, amongst whom we had lived for the last six months.

Cyprus Airways made available office space in East Beirut for the Embassy to operate a basic service. Diplomats and RMP personnel were accommodated in hotels in the Jounieh area whilst the Ambassador, his wife and the CP team commuted daily between the East Beirut and Abey. The Embassy offices were eventually established at the rear of a department store in the eastern suburbs of Beirut with the Ambassador using the residence of a UK businessman in the mountains above East Beirut. During this period, it became impossible for local employees, who lived in West Beirut, to work for the Embassy. Consequently, a CP team member would drive the Ambassador. Visits to West Beirut were undertaken during this period, passing through Israeli checkpoints at the port. The Ambassador's car was greeted in West Beirut with waves from the local population – the British always seemed to be held in high regard! During such visits the Ambassador would visit Yasser Arafat and I am sure that he was acting as a go-between for the Americans and Israelis.

Visit of HRH The Princess Royal to Beirut: Mr (later 'Sir') David Roberts, Her Majesty's Ambassador to the Lebanon with the Princess Royal. Behind the Princess is Chief Inspector Phil Challenger, Metropolitan Police, to his left, SSgt Ken Blake RMP, Cpl Bob Simpson RMP and top right is Cpl Mel Turner RMP.

On 21st August, French paratroopers arrived in Beirut, followed by the US Marines, some Italian Bersaglieri and a squadron of British Cavalry thus forming an international peacekeeping force of some 2,000 men. This force supervised the removal of the PLO, first by ship through the port and then overland to Tunisia, Yemen, Jordan and Syria. Many Palestinian civilians remained in West Beirut.

The Embassy staff and the CP team re-occupied their original residences within West Beirut and the Embassy on the Corniche reopened. Whilst some embassies had suffered considerable damage, we found that the Embassy and our residences, with the exception of the odd broken window, were intact. Life returned to a more normal pattern with the Lebanese Army and Police taking more control of the streets. The Ambassador continued with his daily routine with the weekend spent in Abey and the cool of the mountains.

In September 2002, the Princess Royal visited as President of the Save the Children Fund. The day began at Beirut Airport, where the Ambassador, along with members of the Lebanese Government, greeted her. From the airport, we moved to the Ambassador's residence with the Met Police Protection Officer and the Ambassador's BG in the Ambassador's car with two principals, whilst the Cp team and 2nd Protection Officer formed the PES. In addition, we were accompanied by a platoon of the Lebanese Special Forces assigned to accompany us during the visit.

At the residence, the Princess Royal was introduced to each team member before departing for various schools and the University Hospital in Beirut. The visit was a great success with the Princess being well received wherever she went. At one school, a photographer kept getting too close and was clearly upsetting the Princess. A quick word to the Lieutenant in charge of the SF [Special Forces] platoon and the photographer was whisked away. So impressed was the Princess, she offered the Team Leader a job back in the UK – he explained that unfortunately such treatment would not be tolerated there!

In the 1983 New Years Honours, the Ambassador David Roberts was awarded a Knighthood. This was a great culmination to our tour. He was a pleasure to work for and gave the team unreserved support throughout their tour. The last members of the initial RMP CP team departed the Lebanon on 3rd January 1983. We had come through the experience unscathed and our reputation intact. We had formed an immense fondness for the Lebanese people and were extremely grateful for the loyalty and friendship shown to us by the local staff, some of whom still work for the Embassy to this day."

As part of the British Empire, the East African country of Uganda was described by Winston Churchill as the 'Pearl of Africa'. In 1962, it was granted independence and has since remained part of the Commonwealth. During the 1970s, Uganda was led by Idi Amin, who is known to have supported the Palestinian terrorist group, who hijacked an Air France Airliner by providing the terrorists with a sanctuary at Uganda's main airport at Entebbe. All but four of the hostages on the aircraft were released or finally rescued in the daring Israeli Commando raid 'Op THUNDERBOLT', which has been immortalised in the Film, 'Raid on Entebbe'. Amin's grip on Uganda gradually slipped until the Lord's Rebel Army (LRA) finally got a foothold in the south of the country (not before thousands of men were arrested on suspicion of supporting the anti-government guerilla groups) and Amin fled to Libya. The breakdown of the national government also saw a breakdown in law and order.

The new regime under President Obote became as murderous and autocratic as Amin's with Idi Amin supporters roaming Kampala, setting up illegal road blocks in order to rob and kill the occupants of vehicles. Over the next three years more than 100,000 Ugandans were killed or starved to death. Because of this increased threat, the decision was made to send a RMP CP team to its High Commission in Kampala, the country's capital and, on 14th November 1981, the team deployed, its mission to provide protection to the British High Commissioner and other diplomatic staff supporting the diplomatic mission.

Interestingly, both deployments lasted a year, and as Longmoor was purely a training establishment and although de facto command remained with OC CPW, he also reported to DPM(A) and Comdt RMP Trg Centre, although for a short time command, was managed from 174 Pro Coy RMP for administrative, military and legal reasons. It is widely held that the professionalism of the teams and their ability to integrate into life within the Embassy secured the future of CP with the FCO and RMP CP teams have now been deployed to over 30 trouble-spots around the world affording protection to Heads of Mission and Military Commanders and his/her staff, including operations in areas such as Burundi, the capital of Bujumbura, Darfur in West Sudan and Kabul and Helmand Province in Afghanistan.

In 1982, command of the CP Trg Wing was handed over to Maj Ken Greenland, a former Infantry officer, and the RMP (FCO) Operations Wing was born. The Officer Commanding, was supported by Lt. Col (Ret'd) Steve Manning OBE. A small staff consisting of 1 Warrant Officer (Trg WO), 2 Staff Sergeant Instructors, 1 Sergeant Instructor, 1 Sergeant REME Armourer, 1 Corporal for administration, 1 civilian clerk and 1 typist formed the unit in Kimberley House with two further properties to accommodate teams undergoing training. Operations in NI were still under the control of 177 (Sp) Pl and the training of Officers and NCOs continued in Block 30. Maj Greenland continued his command until he handed over the gauntlet to Maj Adrian Collins, formerly a member of the Parachute Regiment and then Maj PE Farrelly.

The manning of the Operations Wing at the time was an increment of 41 personnel, a number in excess of the Corps training figure, which allowed for five teams of six, each having a reserve team member, the balance allowing for team changeovers.

The agreement between the FCO and MOD was set out in a Memorandum of Understanding (MOU). The deployment request was dealt with by the Director of Military Operations (DMO) in MOD main building. Once an agreement was reached the Ops Wing would be tasked with the training and deployment of the team.

In 1982 Lt Comd Alfredo Ignacio Astiz, (An Argentine naval Officer known as the "Blond Angel of Death"), surrendered to British Forces during the conflict in the Falklands and together with another 151 Argentine military personnel and 39 civilians, was to be repatriated. They were all placed on a ship to the Ascension Islands. However, it transpired that Astiz was wanted by France and Sweden in connection with war crimes carried out during the 'Dirty War';[3] the murder of two nuns and the murder of Dagma Haglin, a 17 year old Swedish girl shot dead in a case of mistaken identity whilst visiting Buenos Aires in 1977. Under pressure from public opinion at home and French and Swedish governments, the UK decided to buy time by putting Astiz on a boat from Ascension to the UK and, while he was in transit, the UK announced he would be made available for interview by representatives of the French and Swedish governments. Soon after, the Argentine government made veiled threats against the welfare of three UK journalists, who had been arrested as spies and linked their release to that of Astiz. The questioning was to be conducted by a Detective Chief Superintendent of the Sussex Constabulary and it was agreed that Astiz would be held at Roussillon Barracks, the home of the Royal Military Police. On Thu 10th June 1982, the ship arrived at Portsmouth and Astiz was met and subsequently escorted to Chichester by Lt Col WR Woods, RMPTC Commandant, WO1 Ewan Grant, Maj Greenland, SSgt Mick Bottomley and Cpl Mick Cowell. After keeping quiet, Astiz was soon repatriated to Argentina, just before the start of the battle for Port Stanley and the Argentine capitulation on 14 June.

In September 1984, on a dusty day in Beirut, the British Ambassador, Mr (later Sir) David Meirs, was paying a courtesy call on his opposite number from the US, the Honourable Reginald Bartholomew at the US Embassy, which was once an apartment block in the non-Islamic East Beirut. He had arrived accompanied by a team of four RMP bodyguards, all Corporals. One Cpl accompanied Sir David to the fourth floor of the Embassy with the

---

[3] The Dirty War (Spanish: *Guerra Sucia*) refers to the state-sponsored violence in Argentina against several thousand left-wing militants, including left-wing revolutionaries, trade unionists, all-out leftist guerrillas and sympathizers, carried out primarily by Jorge Rafael Videla's military dictatorship starting on 24 March 1976, but continuing afterwards until the return to civilian rule in 1983, during which time some 15,000 people died or disappeared. Alfredo Astiz is accused of infiltrating human rights groups, whose members were later kidnapped. The nuns were kidnapped in 1977 and are thought to have been tortured for 10 days before being thrown into the sea from an airplane while still alive, the fate of many of those murdered during the period.

Commander Astiz carrying his kit bag being escorted by Lt Col WR Woods, WO1 Grant, Maj Greenland, SSgt Bottomley and Cpl Cowell.

rest of the team remaining in the car park with the armoured Ford. One of the team, Cpl Rodger, saw that there was a commotion at the front gate to the compound about 100 metres away. A 2½ tonne Chevrolet truck moved through the checkpoint and halted at the barbed wire chicane. Then there was a shot and the truck accelerated towards him. As the vehicle drew level he fired an automatic burst from his HK53 into the driver's side causing the driver to slump at the wheel before the vehicle travelled a further 10 metres before coming to a halt and exploding.

It was calculated that the driver was carrying 2,000 pounds of gas enhanced high explosive and was believed to be heading for the Embassy's underground car park. Had it reached the target the destruction would have been total, the building above having collapsed in on itself. 9 members of Embassy staff were killed, some of whom, who had gone to the windows in response to the initial gun shots, were killed by debris when the windows shattered and furniture and concrete was sent flying in all directions as a result of the explosion.

Cpl Rodger was blown ten meters away as a result of the blast and although mercifully uninjured apart from cuts and bruises, was deafened. The other two members of the CP team fought their way through the dust and rubble in order to find the ambassador having seen their colleague had been blown off his feet. It seemed he was uninjured as he started to coordinate emergency services over his radio via the British Embassy before taking control of the scene of the incident.

Mr Bartholomew had been injured in the blast and Sir David refused to leave until he had been attended by the emergency services. As it happened, it was the CP team that extracted him from beneath the rubble to a vehicle the team had commandeered. Three of the CP team physically carried them out of the building and then escorted both Sir David and Mr Bartholomew to the hospital, their path cleared by Phalange Militia, who fired shots into the air to clear the way.

One member of the CP Team had remained at the scene to co-ordinate the recovery process and remained there until relieved by a British Embassy official.

The following pages show the report sent by the Team Leader, SSgt S R Hardaker, to Longmoor following the bombing and the subsequent Commander-in-Chief's Commendation awarded to the team.

In 1985, following this second major explosion at the US Embassy, Colin Watkins, who was now APM LONDIST revisited Beirut with a Royal Engineer officer with a view of recommending a new embassy and residence for the British Ambassador. An RMP CP team remained in Beirut for the next 17 years when a local team took over the mantle.

The systematic kidnapping of Western civilians began a few years after the Civil War with more than 80 foreigners being taken hostage in Lebanon between 1984 and 1991. Of those taken fourteen were British nationals including Terry Waite, the special envoy of the Archbishop of Canterbury, who was taken on 20 January 1986, and journalist Alec Collett, who was working on behalf of the UN, (his remains were subsequently recovered from the Bekaa valley in 2009, 24 years after his disappearance). On 17 April 1986, journalist John McCarthy was kidnapped whilst on his way to the airport by the militant group, Islamic Jihad. On the same day, three bodies wrapped in blood-stained, white cloth were found on a street near the village of Ruweisat al Sofar, east of Beirut, following a phone call to the Voice of the Mountain radio station controlled by Druze militia in the area. The following day, the three bodies were positively identified as Leigh Douglas, Philip Padfield and an American, Peter Kilburn, who had all been executed possibly in reprisal for British support of US bombing raids on Libya two days previously. This raised concerns regarding the safety of McCarthy. However, on 8th August 1991, he was finally released into the hands of the British Embassy in Beirut and made history as being the longest held hostage in Beirut.

In 1980, Waite first became famous when he successfully negotiated the release of several hostages in Iran. In 1984, he negotiated with Colonel Gaddafi for the release of British hostages held in Libya and again was successful. From 1985, Waite became involved in a number of successful hostage negotiations in Lebanon. However, his use of an American helicopter to travel secretly between Cyprus and Lebanon and his appearance with Colonel Oliver North[4] meant that he was compromised when the 'Irangate'[5] scandal broke. Against advice, Waite felt a need to demonstrate his continuing trust and integrity and his commitment to the remaining hostages. He arrived in Beirut on 12 January 1987 with the intention of negotiating with the Islamic Jihad Organisation, who were holding the men. On 20 January 1987, he agreed to meet with the captors of the hostages as he was promised safe conduct to visit the hostages, who he was informed were ill. The group broke trust and took him hostage on 20 January 1987. Waite remained in captivity for 1,763 days, the first four years of which were spent in solitary confinement.

In November 1988, Cpl (later Major) Martin Pickford deployed to the British Embassy in Beirut along with SSgt Andy Mudd TL, Sgt John Maltby the 2IC and Cpls Glen Roberts, Dave Fairbairn, Paul Lee, Richard Carlyon, Chris Gibson, Mac McDonald and Cpl Mark "Lippy" Lipton. During his tour, rumours abounded and towards the end credible intelligence that Waite was being moved from one safe house to another in west Beirut by means of a fruit truck was received. He was to be immobilised by use of packing tape and laid inside the fruit. The vehicle driver would kill the armed guard as front seat passenger and deliver the truck and Waite to the old Embassy Visa Office at the Shamma Building on the Auto Strada. The team subsequently deployed across the Green Line[6] and took up position at Shamma. At the agreed time

---

4   Colonel Oliver Laurence North (born October 7, 1943) was a US Marine Corps officer at the center of national attention during the Iran-Contra affair during which he was a member of the National Security Council. Currently, he is a political commentator, host of *War Stories with Oliver North* on Fox News Channel, a military historian, and a New York Times best-selling author.
5   The Iran–Contra affair, colloquially known as 'Irangate', was a political scandal in the United States that came to light in November 1986. During the Reagan administration, President Ronald Reagan and other senior U.S. officials secretly facilitated the sale of arms to Iran, the subject of an arms embargo. At least some U.S. officials also hoped that the arms sales would secure the release of hostages and allow U.S. intelligence agencies to fund the Nicaraguan Contras
6   The Green Line was a line of demarcation during the Civil War that separated the mainly Muslim factions in West Beirut from the Christian Lebanese Front in East Beirut. The appellation refers to the coloration of the foliage that grew because the space was uninhabited. Many of the buildings along the Green Line were severely damaged or destroyed during the war.

CONFIDENTIAL

BRITISH EMBASSY
BEIRUT

5 September 1984

See Distribution

VAN BOMB AT AMERICAN EMBASSY: THURSDAY 20 SEPTEMBER 1984

1. At 1100 hours, 20 September 1984, the Close Protection Team consisting of Cpl Rodger NCOIC, Cpls Urwin, Blair, McMichael and Leach were tasked to accompany HMA, Mr H D A C Miers, to an appointment which he had with Mr Reginald Bartholomew, the American Ambassador. On arrival at the American Embassy, normal debus drills were carried out. Cpl Urwin accompanied the Ambassador to the 4th floor to the office of Ambassador Bartholomew. The remainder of the team, including Mr Mohammed Itani, the Ambassador's driver, parked their vehicles in the American Embassy car park and took positions around the Embassy.

2. At approximately 1140 hours, the Team took up standby positions in preparation for HMA's departure. It was at this point that Cpl Rodger noticed a minor disturbance at the north entrance of the American Embassy compound which involved locally-employed security guards of the American Embassy and the driver of a light-coloured Chevrolet-type goods van of the same type used by the American Embassy security staff. This vehicle also carried CD number plates. A few seconds later, the van accelerated out of the chicane towards the Embassy complex. This was followed by a number of shots which were aimed at the vehicle by the locally-employed security guards of the American Embassy. Cpl Rodger, believing the van to contain either a terrorist group or possible explosive device, fired 5 x 5.56 rounds with his HK53 assault rifle which hit the van at the driver's door side and at the same time he saw the driver fall sideways and lose control of the vehicle. The vehicle, out of control, struck a parked Chevrolet security vehicle and it was at this point that the explosion occurred.

3. As a result of the explosion, Cpl Rodger was thrown approximately 10 metres across the car park. Cpls McMichael, Blair, Leach and Mohammed Itani, HMA's driver, who were with their vehicles at the time, were also thrown to the ground.

/Cpl Rodger

CONFIDENTIAL

- 2 -

Cpl Rodger, upon regaining control of his faculties, checked his injuries and found himself to be fully operational. He then proceeded to check the remainder of the Team who, although all suffering from blast deafness, appeared to be in full control of themselves, apart from minor bruises and scratches received during the blast. Cpls McMichael and Blair were directed to ascertain the whereabouts of the Ambassador and his condition. They found the Ambassador and Cpl Urwin inside the American Ambassador's office on the 4th floor. HMA, although suffering from head and facial injuries and severe laceration to the lower right arm, appeared to be in full control of himself and was aware of everything that was happening about him. Cpl Urwin received only a very minor laceration and was assisting HMA with the release of the US Ambassador from under a concrete slab which had fallen across him. On arrival of Cpls McMichael, Blair and Leach in the office, they were able to release the US Ambassador from the debris. Cpls Urwin and Leach removed HMA to a safe location on the ground floor of the Embassy where first aid was administered to him by the Team members. Cpls McMichael and Blair then assisted the US Ambassador out of his room; because of his condition and his personal safety within the building, Cpl McMichael deemed it necessary to carry the US Ambassador to safety to the ground floor, assisted by Cpl Blair, where they were met by the US Ambassador's personal security guards who arranged medical assistance and subsequent admission to hospital.

4. Meanwhile, Cpl Rodger, who had located himself in front of the building, was directing emergency vehicles to the various casualties who were by this time wandering around the complex in states of shock. Due to the fact that both British vehicles had been caught up in the explosion and were write-offs, it was necessary in view of HMA's condition, for Cpl Rodger to commandeer a local civilian driver and his Volvo Estate. With the latter's help, HMA, Cplu Urwin and McMichael plus two other serious civilian casualties were transported to the Abu Jaoude Hospital where HMA was detained for observation and treatment until Saturday 22 September. All Team members were examined at the hospital and were found to be suffering from shock and minor perforation to the eardrums, the worst of these being Cpl Rodger.

5. From the night of 20/21 September, full hospital security was carried out outside HMA's private room until his release on Saturday 22 September. Due to the injuries received by the Team members at the scene, it was deemed necessary to be able to carry out CP role that four CP-trained members were brought over from Cyprus until the injured Team members were fit to carry on the role.

/On

CONFIDENTIAL

- 3 -

On Monday 24 September, Cpls Rodger, McMichael, Blair and Leach were examined by Dr Farid Karam MDFACS, a specialist in the Ear, Nose and Throat Department, who assured the Team members that their injuries were of a temporary nature and that they should receive full hearing within a week. However, Cpls Rodger and Blair, because they had been closer to the scene of the explosion, both received a more serious complaint in their ears; the doctor has informed them that this may result in their ears failing to make a 100% recovery and that Cpl Blair may require an operation. However, only time will tell but their hearing will not be seriously impaired.

6. Mohammed Itani, HMA's driver, also suffered minor bruising to his legs but has recovered since the incident.

7. Both vehicles from the Team - a Ford Minster, fully armour-plated, and the back-up vehicle, a 110 Land Rover - were severely damaged and will no doubt be written off as unoperational. Arrangements are in hand for the use of an armoured Mercedes, on loan from the Australian Ambassador, with the back-up vehicle being a two-door Range Rover. Although an ideal vehicle for the job, it is of limited value due to the fact that it is two-door and alternative transport arrangements are currently being sought. Confirmation from FCO stating a replacement back-up vehicle 110 Land Rover is available, and once all specification requirements are added delivery should be around 2 weeks.

S R BANDAKHR
SSgt
TEAM LEADER

DISTRIBUTION:

External: DPM Army
OC CP Wing RMPTC
Security Department, FCO

Internal: HMA
File 382/1

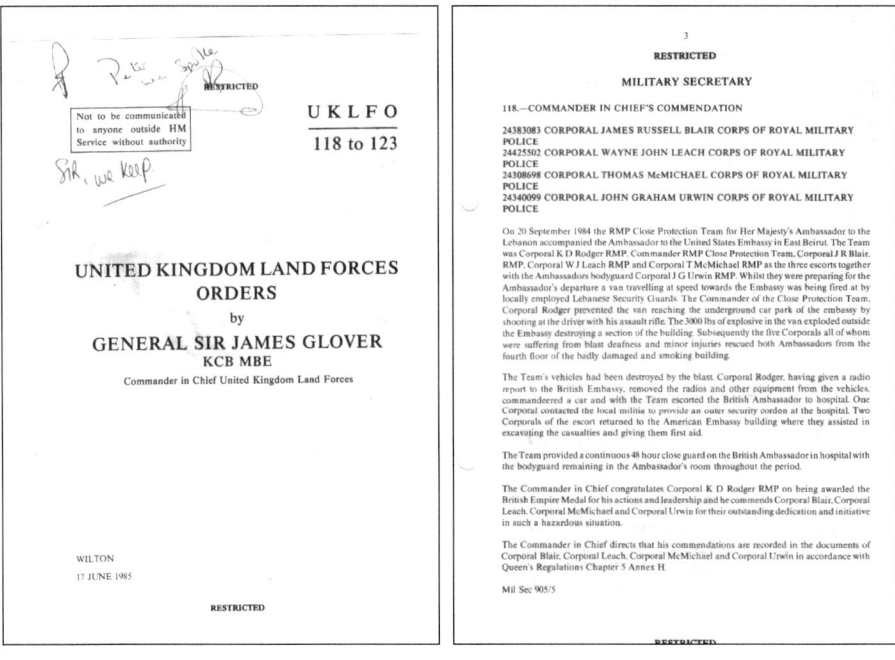

Copy of Commander in Chief's Commendation awarded in response to US Embassy bombing to the RMP CP Team 17 June 1985.

a fruit truck turned up with a driver and body in the front passenger seat. The Ambassador approached the truck and spoke to the driver, who, in turn, opened his jacket to reveal a hand grenade. There was no hostage in the truck and the whole scenario had been orchestrated in order for the driver to gain a new life and identity. The team was left with the decision as to whether they should open fire or not but thankfully the driver was talked down by Myriam, a Lebanese Embassy employee at the Shamma Building. As the team returned to the Embassy, they attempted to cross the green line and found their path blocked by a tank with the barrel levelled directly at them. CP drills are trained and practiced, but it is doubtful they would have proven their worth against a 155mm shell at 25 metres. It is only after such events that teams often realize how tense, and often absurd events can be, and how quickly they can unfold. On completion of that tour with only a couple of days off during the entire six months, the team was extracted by Blackhawk helicopter from the U.S Embassy to Cyprus. In 1990, (following the attack by the IRA that left him with life-changing injuries), SSgt Mudd later received the BEM. However, he credits the team for the award.

In 1991, Sgt Pickford again deployed to Beirut, this time as Team 2IC,

The Cycle of War

These images are of Municipality Street, which crosses Weygand and Foch Street in Beirut. Top left is a postcard image circa 1970, bottom left is a photo taken by Cpl Neil Ashton RMP in 1991, the buildings ravaged by civil war, and the photo below was taken by the RMP CP Team Leader, SSgt Harry Dearing RMP in 2011. The large building that can be seen on the right in all images is the Municipality of Beirut and is an architectural landmark dating back to 1934. Following its restoration, the building was again used as the offices of the Beirut municipal council and Mohafez (administrator). The mosque pictured remained relatively intact for the duration of the war but is hidden in the other pictures by the buildings which were subsequently demolished.

along with the Team Leader, SSgt Bruno Watson and Cpls Steve Smith, Clive Davis, Jim McColgan, Dave "Hippo" Haynes, Eric Fendley and Charlie Fyffe. During the period leading up to Terry Waite's release, there was no confirmation of a release location, which became an issue for the Embassy staff. The CP Team involvement in the release (if in Beirut) was a task given to the Team Leader by the Ambassador, Sir David Tatham. Plans were immediately drawn up between the incoming Team Leader, Chris Richards and Sgt Pickford. The handover and recce phase between the teams were put on hold as preparations for the release took priority. These preparations included the requirement to negotiate the use of a number of armoured vehicles from the German Embassy as the 'cavalcade' for the release would be larger than that enjoyed by the Ambassador. Operational issues such as communication, codes and routes were all priorities as well as the procurement of clothes for the hostages (some of which were donated by members of the CP team) and toiletries for Mr. Waite, who was going to be at the centre of a media frenzy. The team deployed a number of times to the southern suburbs with false hopes of the release of the hostages but, ultimately, it was the Syrian intelligence service "Muhabrahat", who had cleverly secured their release in front of the world's assembled media. The British hostage Jackie Mann was released in Beirut and was brought straight to the Embassy. Sgt Pickford was on Chancery duty that day and he recalls how strange it had been to have met Jackie Mann a couple of days before his kidnap in 1989 and again soon after his release and what the effect that two years in captivity had taken on him.

The Embassy had held Mr. Waite's travel bag and briefcase throughout his incarceration and also, over the years, he had received correspondence from well-wishers all over the world. These items were all forwarded to him following his release in Syria on 18 November 1991.

Cpl (Later WO2) Andy Gibson, who was a member of the CP team under the command of SSgt Chris Richards, met Terry Waite 11 years later at a Remembrance Day Parade, whilst serving at London District. During a conversation between the two, Cpl Gibson recalls that one of his overriding thoughts was that the Size 12 footwear that he donated to Waite prior to his release was at least two sizes too small.

Throughout the civil war in Beirut, unrest continued in Uganda and, by the late 80's, the CP mission in Kampala, the country's capital, was well established as part of the High Commission staff and the wider ex-pat community. The threat in Kampala was not from terrorism but as a result of the breakdown in law and order criminality by rouge rebel army soldiers high on drugs. Although the focus of protection was towards the High Commissioner, in order to respond to this threat, the CP team were unique in that they provided a Quick Reaction Force (QRF) to assist the 20 or so other High Commission staff living in the Diplomatic and Ex-pat quarter of the city.

Pre-Deployment Training at Longmoor had majored quite heavily on the QRF aspect and involved day and night grounds and house clearance drills using distraction grenades (flash bangs), flares and ladders fitted to the roof of a Land Rover 110 to gain access over gates and security fences. Team night vision equipment was limited to one large Common Weapon Sight (CWS) so teams would fashion a holder or clamp to fit D Cell Maglite torches to their personal weapons, a modification which, when discovered by the Ops Wing Chain of Command, was declared an illegal modification.

In 1986, Kampala, capital city of Uganda, had become the centre of an armed power struggle between Yoweri Museveni's government and The Uganda People's Democratic Movement/Army (UPDM/A). The close protection team had been in Kampala since 1982. The violence, however, escalated at an unprecedented speed. Cpl Gerrard was a member of the CP team and was within the residence of six British diplomats, including three women, and had just witnessed the murder of the people who lived next door by rebel African troops. The neighbours, who worked for the country's electricity board, had been marched onto the front lawn and executed by being shot in the back of the head with AK47s. The country was in a state of anarchy so there was no law enforcement in place to offer any protection.

Corporal Gerrard moved every one upstairs securing them behind lockable bars, tossing the keys inside. Armed with an HK 53 and a hundred rounds and his Browning 9mm pistol he positioned himself in the downstairs cloakroom and smashing the small window above the washbasin afforded him an excellent view of the front gate. He covered the area with his rifle and it wasn't long before one of the rebel soldiers started to scale the front gate. As he reached down to retrieve his AK47 from another soldier Cpl Gerrard opened fire and shot the rebel, who fell from the top of the gate. The rebels then retreated to a ditch on the far side of the road and fired an RPG at the house but missed, destroying a tree instead.

Corporal Gerrard radioed the rest of the team, who were located at a second British compound within the city. The rebels continued to fire indiscriminately into the grounds and a small number of rebels had penetrated close to the house, hiding among some trees. There was also a rebel stronghold about a mile away. The team consisting of the Team Leader, SSgt Laffan and three corporals arrived in two armoured Range Rovers and saw that RPGs were still being fired along with small arms fire. The team returned fire and for some minutes a fire-fight between the rebels and CP team ensued. Two of the team remained near the road as the Team Leader and another team member approached the house, and still under fire Cpl Gerrard guided the diplomats from the safe room into the waiting Range Rover. Giving covering fire as they left, the second Range Rover with the remaining two team members followed closely behind.

Some months later, SSgt Laffan, received the Queen's Gallantry Medal in a private ceremony at the HQ 1BR Corps Officer's Mess in Bielefeld, Germany, from the then Lt Gen Sir Peter Inge, who was also the Colonel Commandant

WO2 Andy Gibson and Terry Waite.

of the RMP. The ceremony was conducted privately due to the sensitivities of RMP support to the FCO, which, at the time, was not acknowledged, although a small piece did appear in the satirical magazine 'Private Eye' following a mention of the QGM in the London Gazette. The medal was awarded for 'outstanding leadership, personal example, technical skill and calm direction of the RMP close protection team' and Cpl Gerrard received the Queen's Commendation for Brave Conduct, accompanied by a citation, which spoke of his 'unhesitating courage, devotion to duty and military skills in responding to a serious threat to the lives of civilians ... '

Cpl (later Captain) Kirk Davies deployed as part of one of the many teams that operated in Kampala in 1988. The team's daily routine would include an Individual Bodyguard (IBG) escorting the High Commissioner in his armoured Range Rover with a locally employed driver on his daily program with another team member, who would be appointed as Bodyguard and driver to the High Commissioner's wife on her many charitable visits, as well as her shopping and personal engagements. As always the 'firm base' was provided at the High Commissioner's residence by one of the team supported by the locally employed askaris[7] armed with bow and arrows. On occasions, a Personal Escort Section (PES) or Security Advance Party (SAP) would deploy if travelling outside the city limits but the remaining team members' primary task was as the QRF. The only armoured vehicle was the High Commissioner's Flag car, all the other vehicles, including the teams, were soft-skin Land Rover 110s or 90s. In post, the diplomatic staff could not rely on the local telephone system and each diplomatic property was fitted with a radio base station and each member of staff and their families were issued with radio handsets and a 'RANGER' call sign. Every morning the 'RANGER' call signs would conduct a radio check with the CP team member on residence guard. If no check was forthcoming the team would attempt to raise a response. If this failed the team would deploy to investigate. However, the usual problems in the morning were the house occupant oversleeping or power cuts causing the base stations to close down.

This is not to say that all the team call-outs were uneventful. The team residence was wired with a speaker system, which allowed the radio to be patched through to all the bedrooms. On average a team would be called in the middle of the night at least once a week for some reason or other. This could be over re-action to a simple power cut and backup generator failure or to a genuine call reporting intruders in the grounds attempting to gain access to a house. As can be expected, the team would also find themselves assisting with a number of other situations the diplomatic staff found themselves in, such as vehicle break downs, traffic accidents or domestic fires and accidents. By the start of the 90's, better equipment was starting to be provided for the QRF role and flame proof coveralls, chest rigs, met swivel holsters and Hi Tech magnum boots replaced shorts, fishing jackets, pancake holsters and desert boots. The modified Maglite clamp was still going strong 'under the radar' and finally became team issue some time later.

In calmer times, the teams were able to participate in the work and social life of the High Commission. Team members would be involved in the Sailing Club on Lake Victoria, the Kampala Hash House Harriers, the Christmas Pantomime, as well as accompanying staff on private excursions around the country as much as a sightseer as providing some level of protection. The team

---

7 Askari is an Arabic and Swahili word for 'soldier' and is normally used to describe local troops in East and Northeast Africa serving in the armies of European colonial powers including Great Britain during the period of European rule of East Africa. During both World Wars Askari units served outside the boundaries of their countries of origin.

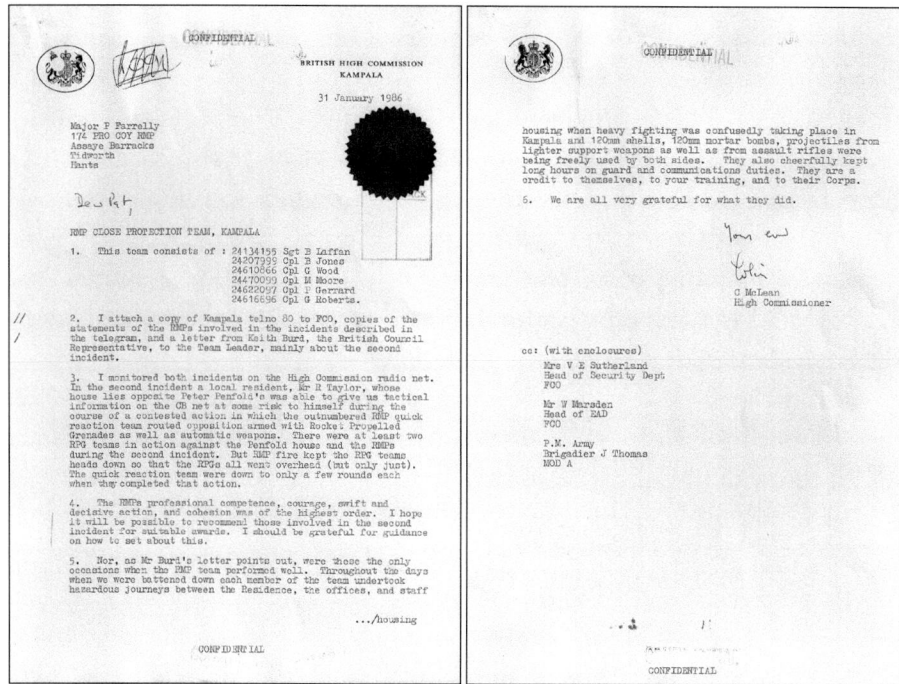

Official correspondence between Colin McLean, British High Commissioner and Maj P Farrelly, following the incident in Khartoum.

also escorted the High Commission 3 ton box lorry on a two day overland trip to the Kenyan High Commission in Nairobi. The lorry, driven by a local driver, had a maximum speed of 50 mph, but due to the poor road conditions on the two day journey rarely achieved 30. The highlights for the lucky team member, were the overnight stay en-route in an old colonial style hotel high in the Kenyan Hills before driving into the Rift Valley before reaching Nairobi and two further nights in a 5 star hotel in the capital. Problems were often encountered in both directions at the border between Kenya and Uganda. Friction between the two countries and border control bureaucracy meant that a 6 hour wait was not uncommon. It says something now of how CP has changed that the trip was made by a single team member with only an overnight bag and a pocket full of Ugandan and Kenyan Shillings to grease a few palms. At a time when mobile phones were still in development, satellite phones were then the domain of SF, the unarmed CP operative was left to get on with it and would possibly have no further contact with another person until arrival at the Kenyan High Commission. These trips were not without drama and problems, but somehow, despite the potholes, the truck would

SSgt Laffan receiving his QGM from Lt Gen Sir Peter Inge, Major Kevin Bacon, OC Spec Ops Unit (G) looks on.

Cpl Gerrard receiving the Queen's Commendation for Brave Conduct from Provost Marshal (British Army of the Rhine) Colonel Geoffrey Taylor.

Typical equipment for CP Teams in Africa. From top: Radio, Fishing Jacket, HK 53 with Maglite torch mount, Browning 9mm Hi Power Pistol, Magazines and clips, 9mm & 5.56mm rounds, Shotgun cartridges, Smoke grenade, illumination flare, distraction grenade, Remington 12 gauge pump action shotgun

always get back with its load and a few more stories from the CP team escort.

Of course it was not 'all work and no play' for the teams. They enjoyed quite a lively social scene amongst the ex-pat and diplomatic community. Although the QRF commitment tours were alcohol free, the team always had an invite to a party in hand. The Kampala Hash Harriers was a running club that was a good way of keeping fit whilst seeing some of the countryside and there was always the opportunity to sail on Lake Victoria. Some team members also tried their hands at landing a famous Nile Perch, a monster fresh-water fish inhabiting Lake Victoria with 30Kg (66lb in old money) examples being caught on a regular basis (it is appreciated that a fisherman has a different perception of size from that of the layman). When not out socialising or at the sailing club, the teams would spend time in the 'gym' on the team house patio pushing weights that were fashioned from scaffold poles and engine parts. As with most military men and women, food and the quality of the cooking was always high on the agenda. The team in Kampala employed a live-in cook,

High Commissioner's Residence, Kampala

who could produce a passable omelet or fish and chips. Saturdays were the cook's night off and so the team would go en mass to the Sheraton Hotel for the evening meal. Not wishing to leave their QRF kit in an insecure location, not even locked in the team Land Rover, the team was readily recognisable and well-known for carrying around large, and heavy sports bags wherever they went and the visits to the Sheraton restaurant were no exception.

The CP team deployment in Kampala lasted 15 years with the CP mission coming to a close in March 1996 with the then OC Ops Wing, Maj Jeremy Green attending a farewell ceremony at the High Commissioner's Residence. At 20 miles from the equator but 3,900 feet above sea level, Kampala provided a pleasant climate to live and work in for almost 30 RMP CP teams.

In January 1997, Sir Richard Branson, the businessman adventurer, accompanied by Per Lindstrand and Alex Richie set off from Marrakech, Morocco, in his trans-global balloon, the Virgin Challenger in an attempt to circumnavigate the world. The balloon reached a height of 30,000 feet when it started to suffer problems with the heat source and envelope. Despite dumping 1300lb of lead ballast, the attempt was doomed to failure and the balloonists had to make a decision; remain at height and attempt a landing in China or cut their losses and land in Algeria, which at the time was in the middle of a civil war. Algeria was chosen and contact was made between the Virgin team

Cpl Kirk Davies astride the equator, a popular photo opportunity for the teams

control room in the UK via the FCO to the Embassy in Algiers. The British Ambassador had a swift meeting with the Minister of Interior, who granted permission to enter Algerian airspace for a landing in the northern Sahara. Amidst the mayhem and phone calls between the Embassy, London and the crew of the balloon, the Ambassador's CP Team Leader SSgt 'Wurze' Young had been asked to assist in the recovery operation and was speaking to the Virgin Team HQ in London, when he asked at what height the balloon was currently and where was it likely to land, oh and by the way was anyone aware that the border was extensively defended by anti tank and personnel mines...a pregnant pause followed and he was told '...we'll get back to you' with the line going dead. A short time later it was confirmed that the balloon had gained height and landed safely approximately 20km inside the Algerian/Morocco border. After having been recovered to the Embassy, they stayed the night with the Ambassador before returning to the UK the next day...minus a balloon. Thanks to SSgt Young they had all their faculties. SSgt Young later became the RSM CPU RMP.

Following a visit by the Director of Military Operations (DMO) in the late nineties, it was highlighted by the OC, Maj Mick Bottomley, that the RMP deployments in support of the FCO had no operational tag, which caused problems, not least of all with the procurement of equipment. Following discussions, the desk officer in charge of operational designations in DMO's

From Left: Joseph (Driver), Cpl Kirk Davies RMP, Lady and Sir Derek March, British High Commissioner, relaxing on hills overlooking Kampala

Dept, Military Operations (MO) 2, and the OC (based on the DS he had working with him at the time) chose the name 'BANDOG'. The dictionary definition of 'bandog' or 'baendog' states, "A bandog was achieved by the coupling of a rottweiler and a pit-bull terrier" and is now the operational name for all FCO deployments abroad.

It is a common misconception that RMP Close Protection teams operate and deploy together throughout their career out of an HQ somewhere in middle England. This is not the case. On completion of the Close Protection Course, successful students return to their respective units around the world. When they get the 'call' from the Ops staff at CPU, individually they arrive at Longmoor on a predetermined day to undergo Pre Deployment Training (PDT) and it is then they meet up with the other team members with whom they are going to spend the next 6-9 months. It is often the case that they would not have met each other before and each will have a different level of experience to bring to the operation. The following three weeks spent on PDT is designed to foster team cohesion, update individuals on theatre specific SOPs whilst ensuring shooting standards are attained as well as assessing an individual's mental and physical well being (often teams can be left in isolation for periods of time). The following article written by SSgt Joe Lincoln gives an idea of what it is like to receive the 'call' followed by deployment:

The Royal Military Police Journal (August 1999)

AN RMP TEAM LEADER'S VIEW

I am summoned to the RSM's office – a signal has arrived proclaiming that I have been selected as the Team Leader of a RMP CP Team assigned to provide protection for a VIP in Africa. Now I have to go through the system.

This starts with Pre Deployment Training (PDT) at CPU and usually takes three weeks. As leader, I am responsible for moulding the team and preparing it for deployment. Each team member will have various responsibilities such as 'Q', Team Medic, Communications NCO, G2 NCO etc. PDT instructors will normally have been leaders themselves and will help in the preparation. Staff Sergeants Levick and Rees were my instructors and ensured we all felt fully prepared for everything. The training acts both as a refresher for initial CP skills and more importantly to learn enhanced CP specific-to-post skills. Part of my training for post was with SF in the use of some amazing nautical craft – some resembling something from the latest star war movies.

Deployment to post is staggered to allow handover/takeover of the various responsibilities to be carried out. The means of deployment will vary, depending on location. My team deployed by plane, train and ferry. Dates were condensed because of a flight controller's strike. This meant that PDT finished on the Thursday and I, my 2IC, Q and one other team member flew out on the Friday. To be a CP operative will mean an understanding wife or girlfriend is essential.

On arrival in post, we were met by SSgt Mark Guest, the leader I was replacing. During our drive from the airport, all looked normal and peaceful, but this was a superficial view and concealed significant underlying problems that I would see firsthand in the following days. The CP team is accommodated in a villa where we have a manned 24-hour ops room and an excellent gym. Sky TV allows contact with what is happening in the outside world. For the next few days my team arrived and Mark's team left. The changeover was carried out as effectively and efficiently as possible without interfering with the team's operational commitments.

Operational commitments in post – why have a CP team? Make no mistake this is one of the most dangerous countries in the world. Without our presence, the VIP and his staff could not be here. Our VIP travels everywhere in a fully protected armoured car and following behind is the Personal Escort Section (PES) in a vehicle that is also armoured. Gun ports allow us to provide covering fire from the vehicle without breaking the seal. Tactical driving is carried out wherever the VIP goes, but a degree of common sense has to be applied, as the locals are not the best drivers in the world! It is generally better to avoid traffic accidents as an immobilised vehicle is of no use. Having said that, it depends on the particular situation at hand because the safety of the VIP is paramount.

In conclusion, as I write these notes I have been in post for two months. The team works well together and we are into the 'routine' (not a great CP word!). I cannot imagine a more fulfilling job and I feel privileged and lucky to be in the command of such a dedicated and professional team of men. If anyone in GPD land is considering Close Protection as a specialisation, then my advice is GO FOR IT!!! If you have what it takes, you will not regret it.

CPU has developed excellent relations with other agencies and organisations. I felt proud to share in the professionalism of CPU and felt that RMP was represented in a most favourable light. Successful completion of PDT is not a foregone conclusion. As well as completing it, other criteria have to be met. As leader, I had to examine my team and myself in close liaison with the DS and satisfy CPU and myself that the team, under my command, is the best to provide protection for our designated VIP. If selected, this group of men deploy to an area of the world where, in certain areas, life expectancy for an unescorted European was six and a half minutes! To be away from friends for six months with no R&R can be a daunting prospect. However, as with most tasks we are presented with, the adversity is dispensed and the NCOs concentrate on the job in hand to highest standards possible.

2007 saw an escalated threat in Khartoum, Sudan and a five man CP Team lead by SSgt (later WO1) Richard Keightley deployed from the Close Protection Unit to afford protection to the Ambassador, Dr Rosalind Marsden. On Monday 26th November, following a complaint from a member of staff at Unity School in Khartoum, Mrs Gillian Gibbons, a British national working at the school, was arrested following allegations that she had insulted the Prophet Mohammed by naming a teddy bear after him. This caused a diplomatic incident involving politicians at the highest level from both the United Kingdom and Sudan and two MPs from the UK came to Khartoum to assist in the negotiations for the release of Mrs Gibbons.

Unfortunately, the incident received massive global media coverage and, as a result, Khartoum saw civil unrest and threats against Mrs Gibbons.

One afternoon, Sgt (later SSgt) Lloyd Paterson, the team 2IC was in the Embassy keeping an eye on the Ambassador when, on looking outside, he saw approximately 8,000 demonstrators wielding all manner of knives, machetes and spears all vying for the death of Mrs Gibbons, who was secured in a police station a few miles away. Sgt Paterson quickly informed Dr Marsden to stay away from the windows and contacted Sgt Paul Burton, who had secured the Ambassador's residence that was located within the Embassy grounds but overlooked the road. Sgt Burton's reaction to the crowd was one of mild surprise to say the least and he quickly armed himself with everything he could lay his hands on. The Team Leader accompanied by Sgt Jon Ashley, a RAF policeman, attended the scene in an armoured Toyota Land Cruiser and monitored the crowd from about 150m away whilst keeping Sgt Paterson and Sgt Burton up-to-date as events unfolded. The remaining member of the team Sgt David Reynolds was on standby at the team house to facilitate the rescue of the rest of the team should the worst happen (it is widely held that plan would have been highly innovative).

After a short while, it transpired that the main motivation of the crowd was to deliver a Letter of Displeasure to the Embassy and it was decided that Mr Russell Philips, Head of the Consular and Visa Section, would receive the letter with Sgt Paterson escorting him to the Embassy gates. As the two approached the baying crowd, SSgt Keightley and Sgt Ashley saw a breakaway group of five people run towards a pickup truck. As the two members of the CP team thought the worst, they were exiting the vehicle with weapons drawn to deal with whatever threat manifested. At the crucial moment, the five marauders produced some extremely dangerous-looking drums and tambourines and rejoined their fellow 'revellers' in a rather jovial mood. Sgt Paterson, meanwhile, approached the gate with Mr Philips and the letter was accepted. Soon afterwards the crowd dispersed and after much wrangling it was agreed that Mrs Gibbons could return to the United Kingdom and, on Monday 3rd December, Mrs Gibbons joined a flight back to the United Kingdom, accompanied by Mr Phillips, Lord Ahmed (Head of the Muslim Council of Great Britain), Baroness Warsi (then the Conservative Shadow Minister) and a member of the Ambassador's Close Protection Team.

As a result of the management of the incident by the UK mission in Khartoum, the Right Honourable David Miliband MP, Secretary of State for Foreign and Commonwealth Affairs sent a letter of thanks to the Ambassador, in which he cited the CP team.

SUPPORTING THE FCO 137

The situation in Khartoum remained volatile and on 14th September 2012, the CP Team were again involved an incident, which, thanks to their actions, undoubtedly saved lives. Below is the report sent by the Team Leader, Capt Steve Tickner RMP back to Longmoor following demonstrations in the capital. A Californian made film that insulted the Prophet Mohammad, incensing the Muslim community worldwide. In Libya, two days before, the U.S consulate was attacked resulting in the deaths of the U.S. Ambassador and three other Americans. Demonstrators attacked the German Embassy, which is next to the British Embassy in Khartoum, setting it on fire before attempting to gain entry into the British Embassy.

Place: BE Khartoum.
Date: 14 Sep 12.
Time: Between 1435 – 1525 hrs
Incident timeline:
1435 hrs: Large demonstration 1000 + forms up outside BE South gate and German Embassy in order to demonstrate against the Germans. Crowd throws rocks and other material at both embassies. BE guards move from outer cordon into inner cordon.
1440 hrs: Crowd dispersed by Sudanese Police, who use tear gas.
1445 hrs: Crowd returns continue to throw rocks and breech the BE outer vehicle gate.
1450 hrs: Crowd enter BE vehicle checking area and start to attack the inner gate. Sudanese Police had not formed any barrier so the gate could have been breached within minutes. I therefore decided to use Smoke Signal and distraction grenades to remove the threat and deter the crowd from entering the inner compound. I threw 2 x Smoke and 2 x distraction and Sgt Stagg threw 1 x smoke and 1 x Distraction. The area cleared immediately and the Police appeared to have formed an effective barrier in the location of the destroyed gate (outer gate).
1455 hrs – 1500 hrs: The Sudanese Police line appeared to dissolve again and the crowd entered the vehicle search area and started throwing stones and missiles again. They then started crossing the Hesco perimeter wall leading to the German Embassy. The demonstrators start to cause damage to the German Embassy, whilst missiles and rocks continued to be thrown at the BE.
1505 hrs: Demonstrators open the gate leading from the German Embassy

to the British Embassy and have free access to the BE internal compound. I threw 2 x smoke and 2 x distractions and Sgt Stagg threw 1 x distraction to deter further penetration. Unfortunately, individuals continued to attempt entry to the BE inner compound, therefore, a decision was made to fire 1 x warning shot, which I fired into the sand located at the top of the Hesco wall. Sgt Stagg witnessed the shot and there were no injuries caused as a result. The Police seemed to gain control of the situation again and the protestors were pushed back. However, they remained in the German Embassy causing more damage and lighting a number of fires. There were two more attempts to enter the BE inner compound via the gate. However, they were stopped by the use of smoke and distraction. I threw 2 x Distraction and 1 x smoke. One demonstrator attempted to grab a deployed smoke grenade but ran away as soon as he touched the smoke grenade.

1525 hrs: Sudanese Police clear the German Embassy of demonstrators. Local fire service start to fight the fire.

1740 hrs: OSM confirms that the Embassy situation is now secure.

Injuries: Non suspected

Future action: Team will uplift the HMA, who was on a different engagement, and return him to his residence. A CP rep will then stay at his Res until the situation calms down.

In conclusion: The team did an excellent job and remained professional and composed throughout. The OSM was present in the Embassy throughout the incident and thanked the team for their efforts.

As a result, the Team received letters of thanks from both the Chief of the Defence Staff and the Permanent Under Secretary of State seen on the following page.

Two years later, Capt Jim Devenney RMP was Team Leader in Kabul, Afghanistan, responsible for the British Ambassador. On 27th April 2008, the Ambassador, Sir Sherard Cowper Coles KCMG LVO, and other dignitaries were the guests of President Karzai at the Mujahedeen Victory Day being held at the Ghazni Stadium in the city. The focus of the celebrations was a military parade with the President taking the salute before a 21 gun salute. The salute was the trigger for an attack against the parade and, although it is believed that some type of explosive was used, the salute masked the noise. Small-arms fire could be heard at the opposite end of the pavilion and when the Afghan Security Forces began to react it became apparent that it was not part of the programme. Due to restrictions imposed by local security, only individual bodyguards were permitted to escort their respective principals, the teams waiting some 150m away. Capt Devenney appointed himself as BG for that day, but his duty was hampered further by him being placed 5 rows of seats away from the Ambassador. What follows are the accounts of that incident by both the Ambassador and Capt Devenney's post-incident report:

My life literally depended on my Royal Military Police Close Protection Team. The whole team had turned out for the patrol with the Coldstream guards, wearing, unusually for them, battledress (they normally wore civilian clothes). Later, I was often to meet former members of my team, similarly dressed, working for a senior officer. That spring, however, they were to face their greatest test.

In the weeks before the big parade, President Karzai discussed arrangements several times with the war cabinet. It was obvious that he was worried. He told the Afghan Defence Minister, General Wardak, that he wanted to spend as little time as possible in the open air. He suggested moving the ceremonies from the parade ground to the more confined space of the Olympic stadium nearby. He quizzed General Wardak on how long he would have to spend inspecting troops. He asked others to confirm that adequate security arrangements had been made.

The Embassy's security advice was that there was a risk of an attack at the parade. My new Close Protection Team had changed over only a day or two before. The new team leader, Captain Jim Devenney of the Royal Military Police, had long experience of these things. He made clear that he was worried about me attending the parade. Initially, I accepted their advice: I would stay away. But then I discovered that the American Ambassador and most of the diplomatic corps were going to be there. It would be noticed if the British Ambassador, alone of the more prominent ambassadors, stayed away. And, if an incident did occur, there would be Afghan conspiracy theories about the British having had advance warning, and perhaps even having been involved. So I concluded that I had no option but to attend. I reasoned that the Americans would have taken every possible precaution. Moreover, Karzai's 800-strong Presidential Protective Service was highly competent – and American mentored.

As was usual with events at which Karzai was present, the area was secured days in advance, and outside guests were expected to turn up hours

General Sir David Richards GCB CBE DSO ADC Gen

Chief of the Defence Staff

D/CDS/2/2/1

Zone D
5th Floor
Ministry of Defence
Main Building
Whitehall
London SW1A 2HB
United Kingdom

Telephone	+44 (0)20 721 83353 Principal Staff Officer
	+44 (0)20 721 86031 Staff Officer
Facsimile	+44 (0)20 721 86799
DFTS	9621 + ext
E-mail (Mil)	CDS-PrivateOffice
Email (Civ)	CDS-PrivateOffice@mod.uk

Brig Edward O Forster-Knight OBE
Headquarters Provost Marshal
Ramillies Building IDL 431
Marlborough Lines
Monxton Road
Andover
Hampshire
SP11 8HJ

September 2012

Dear Eddie,

I would like to extend my personal thanks to Captain Steve Tickner and the Royal Military Police team on duty at the British Embassy, Khartoum. They have demonstrated what those of us fortunate enough to work with you have always known: dedication, restraint and professionalism.

Their courageous actions not only protected the Embassy and the staff but did so without causing loss of life and without enflaming the situation further. Action of this kind, in the face of such provocation and while the German Embassy was engulfed next door, demonstrates the highest traditions of the British Army.

I would be grateful if you would pass on my heartfelt congratulations and gratitude for their actions to Captain Tickner and his team. The RMP CPU can be equally pleased.

Great stuff !

Yours ever,

David

As a result, the Team received letters of thanks from both the Chief of the Defence Staff and the Permanent Under Secretary of State.

Foreign & Commonwealth Office

Brigadier Edward O Forster-Knight OBE
Headquarters Provost Marshal
Ramillies Building IDL 431
Marlborough Lines
Monxton Road
Andover
Hampshire
SP11 8HJ

Simon Fraser CMG
Permanent Under-Secretary of State
Foreign & Commonwealth Office
King Charles Street
London
SW1A 2AH

Tel: 020 7008 2150
Fax: 020 7008 3776
Email: pus.action@fco.gov.uk
www.fco.gov.uk

[by post]

27 September 2012

Dear Brigadier,

ASSISTANCE IN KHARTOUM

On behalf of the Foreign and Commonwealth Office, and in particular colleagues in our Embassy in Khartoum, I would like to thank the Royal Military Police (RMP) team for their efforts and support during the recent demonstrations in the Republic of Sudan. The attack on the compound housing the British and German Embassies was not contained by local police forces and it was only because of the quick actions of your team that Embassy staff on the compound were kept safe and damage to British assets was kept to a minimum.

As you may imagine, we in the FCO spent a good deal of last week focussed on ensuring the safety and security of all UK Government staff overseas. I am very grateful and glad that the RMP team in Khartoum were involved and able to play such a vital and professional role.

early. Although my bodyguards tended to take such instructions literally, I knew from experience that one needed to be there only sixty minutes or so in advance. So that morning, Sunday 27 April 2008, we arrived in the stand reserved for foreign VIPs at 8a.m. and had to wait only until 9.15a.m. before the President appeared.

I spent the hour gossiping in the sun with other guests. The ISAF Commander, General McNeill, was there with a clutch of other senior officers, including the training mission commander, Major General Bob Cone. Among them were several British officers, including my Defence Attaché, Colonel Simon Newton, in dress uniform, wearing the dark-green beret of his regiment and a Sam Browne. Most ambassadors were there. Among those on the front row alongside me were the American, Bill Wood; the charming and able Canadian, Arif Lalani; and the immensely civilized Frenchman, Régis Koetschet, whom the French Foreign Minister Bernard Kouchner was shortly to move.

I took photographs of my colleagues. My fellow amateur photographer, COMISAF's Executive Officer Trevor Bredenkamp, and I lazily took snaps of each other.

My mind flashed back to another parade ground, at another time: to Cairo, on 6 October 1981, the annual October War victory parade. With the world watching, Islamist terrorists dressed as soldiers had leapt from the military truck on which they were passing the saluting base, and pumped 40 Kalashnikov rounds into President Anwar Sadat. Many others had been killed or wounded. My first Ambassador, Sir Michael Weir, had narrowly escaped being hit. A great friend in the Austrian Embassy had been badly injured. I had been watching the parade on television in the Embassy and had seen the screen suddenly go blank. I wondered whether, thirty years later, history was going to repeat itself.

In front of us, the lines of Afghan soldiers stood in the sun, awaiting the arrival of their Commander-in-Chief. Their tasseled shakoes and high boots gave the whole assembly a slightly comic air. For security reasons, none of them carried a single bullet for their ancient rifles. The only armed personnel were those around the perimeter of the parade ground, including the Presidential Protective Service snipers.

Eventually, there was movement to the north. The Presidential motorcade rolled on to the parade ground and passed before us, with Karzai standing tall in the back of a camouflaged humvee. From the southern end of the ground the Defence Minister, my friend General Abdul Rahim Wardak, rolled forward in his humvee, to greet his Commander-in-Chief. General Wardak's uniform was a sight to behold. With a steeply raked Russian-style cap, his sunglasses and a chest load of medals, he looked a cross between a marshal of the Soviet Union and a Latin American dictator. He wheeled round and drove alongside the President as they passed in their humvees up and down the lines of soldiers. The motorcade stopped in front of the reviewing platform, fifty yards to the north of our stand. President Karzai and his party dismounted and took their places on the stand. The band struck up, we rose and stood to attention as the Afghan National Anthem was played.

As the dying bars of the Anthem faded away, I heard a faint crackling sound from across the parade ground. After a second or so I realized it was gunfire. I assumed that some sort of rifle salute was being mounted and tried to see where it was coming from. It was then that I spotted the commandos of the Presidential Protective Service sprinting on to the parade ground, falling prone and starting shooting towards the south.

All hell broke loose. Screams, shouts, panic. The Afghan Army lined up on the parade ground broke ranks and fled, flinging their empty rifles to the ground, the tassels of their shakoes swinging up in the air. I spotted General McNeill taking cover. Others around me dropped on to their hands and knees and crawled behind the low concrete parapet that separated us from the parade ground proper. All around the Afghans guarding the perimeter were opening fire, with bullets whizzing through the air in every direction.

Suddenly, I felt a pair of hands on my shoulders, and a voice in my ear. 'Come with me, Sir,' said Jim Devenney, as he swung me round and frogmarched me up the steps and out of the back of the stand. There the position was, if anything, more dangerous than in front, as the Afghan perimeter guards seeming to be firing almost at random into and on to the parade ground. Jim gripped me to one side of him, saying that he had to put his body between me and incoming fire.

We raced, or rather stumbled, towards the exit. Suddenly, I spotted the American Ambassador's armoured Land Cruiser inside the perimeter fence. I banged on the window. Bill Wood's bodyguard nearly shot me, but Bill levered open the door and told me to get in quickly. I did so, and was never more grateful to be inside an armoured vehicle. We sped off, scattering the crowds as we lurched and pitched over the rough ground to the gate. I had lost Jim and assumed he had got into the second American vehicle. But I owed my life to him, and to Bill Wood.

Excerpt from *Cables from Kabul, The Inside Story of the West's Afghanistan Campaign* by Sir Sherard Cowper-Coles, published by Harper Press

By the time, I managed to get forward to HMA, he was already lying down in cover. I communicated with the VIP car to standby, as an evacuation was imminent. Chaos ensued and I grabbed HMA from the rear and afforded him body cover as I forced him through the crowd toward the small doorway exit at the rear of the pavilion. I was aware of small arms fire increasing as we exited the pavilion into the rear area.

Maintaining body contact with HMA, we were forced down against a wall in cover briefly until I identified our next bound. At this stage, I had no communications with the vehicles. There seemed to be gunfire everywhere around, some of which was within metres of HMA. We moved forward 15m, at which point the US Ambassador was embossing as the American security had forced a vehicle inside the controlled area. Shouting to the American BG, I moved HMA forward and put him inside the vehicle with the American Ambassador. I escorted the vehicle on foot (also using it as cover) until it was clear of the crowd and I had arrived at my pre-arranged pick-up point. My driver was forcing the VIP vehicle through the panicked crowd and increasing traffic. I called to the two PES members, who had deployed on to the ground to emboss immediately and we shadowed the US Ambassador's vehicle back to the US Embassy. We gained control of HMA once within the US compound and returned immediately to the British Embassy before the city was locked down.

Capt Jim Devenney RMP CP Team Leader

Thankfully, HMA was uninjured and, in a private conference later that day, he thanked Capt Devenney [and the team] for remaining calm and professional throughout and praised the Team's efforts. He publicly acknowledged to his staff that he would not have been so lucky had the Team not been there.

Following an investigation it transpired that there was up to 6 attackers, who were members of the Taleban using small arms and rocket propelled grenades. Although they were not close enough to target effectively, they managed to kill at least one civilian and a Member of Parliament. 11 people were wounded, including two local police officers and a further Member of Parliament. Three insurgents were killed, but three escaped.

Capt Devenney went on to become the Training Officer at the Close Protection Unit. Not one for sitting still, on the 19th January 2010, he led a team of eight to Haiti following an earthquake that left an estimated 200,000 people dead and over 1 million homeless. As is common with disasters of this scale, the threat of looting and violence increased and the team were responsible for the safety of the British Ambassador, (based in Santo Domingo), Steven Fisher and a Rapid Response Team, who were assisting in the relief effort. The following is a short account written by Capt Devenney for the RMP Corps Journal:

12 Jan 2010 saw an earthquake of 7.0 magnitude hit the Caribbean isle of Haiti with an epicentre 10 miles west of Port-au-Prince. In minutes, 3 million people were in dire need of emergency aid in terrible conditions.

The High Readiness Team (HRT) at CPU are used to deploying at short notice, and when assistance was requested from the Foreign and Commonwealth Office (FCO) to gain safe access to Haiti for their Rapid Deployment Team (RDT) the Ops staff went into overdrive. Christened Op LIMHILL by MOD, planning and preparation began in earnest. The criminal threat was deemed to be high, following the collapse of the jail. The escape of hundreds of prisoners coupled with the deteriorating security situation due to a weakened police force meant that aid agencies were at risk. Consequently, eight operatives deployed on a nine day mission to the country, led by the CPU Training Officer, Captain Jim Devenney. Just thirty-six hours after the initial call, the HRT team were waiting to board.

Gaining the authority to deploy 8 troops with weapons and ammo was proving a challenging diplomatic process. The team were en route to the US when, literally at the last minute, the green light was given to continue to the start line in Santo Domingo.

Arriving in Santo Domingo, the HRT went straight to meet the British Ambassador, HMA Steven Fisher. The Embassy had procured three four-wheel drives and a small truck to ferry the RDT and HRT the twelve hour journey across the island. As the initial brief and welcome began, news came of further after-shocks in the earthquake zone.

After an overnight stop en-route and chaos at the border, the two teams were finally into Haiti. As the hastily-assembled convoy drew closer to the city, they saw evidence of what lay ahead – a collapsed bridge, traffic building

HMA Kabul, Sir Sherard Cowper-Coles KCMG LVO, with SSgt 'Flash' Hannan RMP (wearing sunglasses) keeping an eye open.

up with aid trucks going in and the afflicted coming out, escaping the ruins behind them. There were more and more people on the streets, crudely painted signs begging for food and the general stench of a city in distress.

The teams pressed on and the banter, which had kept spirits up on the long journey, suddenly ceased as the true level of devastation became apparent. They found themselves transiting silently through the worst hit downtown areas amongst precarious ruins, partially collapsed homes, smashed vehicles and a population in disbelief.

An impromptu drive around the city before locating the airport served as stark reminder of the task that lay before them. HRT would be responsible for escorting the ambassador to various appointments in and around the city and also protecting the RDT in their search for any surviving British nationals needing consular assistance. With only rudimentary mapping of a city now in ruins and no local knowledge – the team had their work well and truly cut out for them.

HRT had deployed to be self-sufficient for up to 7 days and made camp in the only remaining real estate at the UN compound – next to the runway. The airport was operating around the clock with relief aid aircraft arriving and departing constantly. The team made themselves as comfortable as possible – yet sleep would be hard to find in more than 20 minute portions.

With two distinct tasks, the eight man CP team split into two smaller teams – one dedicated to HMA under Capt Devenney, and the second assigned to the RDT under SSgt Lloyd Paterson.

The ambassador had a number of diplomatic events to attend – including the local government morning meetings with the Haitian President (now being conducted in the courtyard of one of the remaining police stations with his tattered administration seated on plastic garden chairs). With London calling for information, the HRT escorted the ambassador on a city trip for him to assess and report the scale of the damage. He would visit a temporary hospital, a Red Cross centre in the small town of Léogane (30km west of the capital and equally as devastated) and a US Marine food distribution point. Strange how some structures around the city had survived virtually unscathed but others in the same street had been completely destroyed. And although the Haitians had suffered a disaster of epic proportions, had lost loved ones, had little food, water or access to medical supplies, they faced their hardships with dignity, queuing for aid and trying to restore some semblance of normality in the face of near chaos.

The RDT had compiled a list of UK expatriates thought to be living in Haiti and set off with their CP team to try and locate any Brits, whom they might be able to help. With a number of 'last known addresses' the challenge for the team was to locate streets that simply weren't there anymore and make sure that the FCO workers were safe, while they set about making enquiries. Rewardingly, many of the names on the list were found alive and well, the majority of whom had decided to stay and pick up their adopted lives. Quite by accident, the team stumbled upon a convent that had been offering basic relief run by two Irish Sisters. They were desperately in need of supplies and with what extra medical supplies and water were to hand – the convent was offered some re-supply. Again – although the threat of emerging criminality was rising as the escaped convicts returned to their stomping grounds and general desperation increased, the team were allowed to go about their business – and only on the last day of the deployment was a relief worker and driver shot and killed in the city.

The RDT were only scheduled to be in post for 7 days and the FCO took the decision not to replace them as they had achieved what they could. It was up to the HRT to break camp and plan the recovery to Santo Domingo. Once clear of the city and with the task complete, the team could enjoy the fantastic scenery around them throughout Haiti and the Dominican Republic – endless palm fields, jungle covered mountains and the glistening border lake, Azuei.

Op LIMHILL was a step out of the norm for the HRT, used to tasks in Iraq or Afghanistan, CPU RMP demonstrated that they could mount incredibly short notice operations into unfamiliar territory and situations. Op LIMHILL was an opportunity to showcase the ability of the Unit to react and deliver – rightly deserving its reputation as a global leader in the provision of protective services.

CP teams that have deployed in support of the FCO have received many plaudits along the way, and the following are examples of the feelings felt by their Principals towards them. The first piece written by Her Majesty's Ambassador Sir AJ Ramsay stems from 1990 adorns the walls of Kitchener House and the latter a short piece written in 2010 especially for this history by Mr Mark Sedwill, previously Her Majesty's Ambassador to Afghanistan before being appointed as the NATO Senior Civilian Representative in Afghanistan, a Four Star diplomatic appointment. Despite the passing of 10 years between each, the message remains the same.

> Members of my Close Protection Team occasionally lent me a copy of the Corp Journal. I read it with great interest and am repeatedly struck by the diversity of tasks the Corps undertakes. No mention, however, has yet been made of the arduous and dangerous work its members carry out here. This article is an attempt to fill that gap whilst placing on record my own appreciation and that of my colleagues, and my wife, of the skill, courage and dedication to duty of the teams that have served in Beirut, and to those who select, train and support them.
>
> There is no denying the demanding nature of the work. As the 'Principal' I know this better, I suppose, than anyone else. It is a 24 hours a day job, 7 days a week, carried out in unprecedentedly dangerous circumstances. I doubt if there is anywhere in the world with the same wide mix of threat at the same persistently high level. One cannot assume that any one part of Beirut is necessarily going to be safer than another. So the job demands constant alertness. No two days in Beirut are the same, and the security situation can change devastatingly quickly and quite without warning. Cumulatively, this imposes a considerable strain on even the most experienced NCO. Last year, it was exacerbated by the threat of almost daily shelling, sometimes lasting for four to six hours at a stretch, often during the night, which in turn presented added problems of maintaining a high level of professional alertness when short of sleep.
>
> As I hope those who have served would agree, there are compensations.

The devastation in Haiti was total

The knowledge that the team in indispensible to our remaining here is one; without their protection we would have packed up years ago. They, therefore, make a direct and real contribution to maintaining a British diplomatic presence in an uneasy but vital part of the world in which important UK interests are directly engaged. Second, there is the pleasure of putting into practice, for real, the skills acquired in training and in previous experience elsewhere. This may help to explain the uniformly high standard among the teams it has been my privilege to know here. Third, there is the variety; the bizarre combination and contrast of life in Lebanon. The tempo of life here almost never slackens. The Lebanese are still a hospitable and friendly people and the curious ability British soldiers have for getting on with foreigners earns the team respect, admiration and friendship. They are, in that respect, probably rather better ambassadors than I am, since their contacts are free of all protocol and prejudices, which tend to be directed at someone in my position. Last, but by no means least, is the pleasure and privilege of working with Lebanese colleagues of the highest motivation. It has always been a most harmonious and rewarding relationship for both sides.

I suppose the greatest tribute I can pay the CP teams of my time here is to say that I never worried about my security; never for one moment felt they would not give their best, nor felt that I was other than in safe hands. That is not to say that we have not been more at risk at some times than others. The nature of the job here makes that unavoidable. I am conscious too that where my own life had been at risk, that is all the more true of theirs. Constant risk and exposure to date have the same effect of attrition as any other persistently disagreeable phenomenon (even agreeable ones – one would get bored with champagne and caviar if one's diet consisted of little else).

But attrition has never had any noticeably lowering effect on morale or professionalism. Stamina and a high heart seem the essential qualities for Beirut. Off duty, the CP team reveal a range of rare talents – caricature and cooking to name but two. I have only once eaten a better curry in my life. No doubt the last owes a great deal to the example of the wives, mothers and girlfriends. The separation involved in a Beirut posting is never easy for families. This became all too clear last year, when anxieties about security and the shelling were made worse by lurid media treatment. I realise now, from our own experience, that families had a much tougher time than we did. It is they, quite as much as husbands, fathers and boyfriends who serve here, who are the real heroes, or heroines, rather, in case I should be accused of chauvinism.

AJ Ramsay CMG Former HMA to Lebanon.

I wasn't new to having a bodyguard when I arrived in Afghanistan. Indeed, having spent a couple of years in Pakistan with a young Pashtun from the border areas, whose gaze contained generations of vendetta should anyone even flirt with harming me, I was ready for the experience. Or so I thought.

I first came to Afghanistan in February on a recce for my tour as British Ambassador, which was to begin a few weeks later. Kabul in winter is a bleak collage of rubble, mud and snow. I arrived on a commercial flight from Dubai and wandered down the aircraft steps into the terminal building. For those who haven't been ambassadors – and I hadn't – this was fine. In some countries one is met at the aircraft, in others at the immigration desk and in a few having passed through all the way through to the exit. So I just joined the immigration queue. This being Afghanistan, where the security industry is ubiquitous, the queue consisted mostly of beefy American ex-servicemen with luxuriant and often extravagant facial hair. Suddenly, I noticed a podgy Afghan (whom we later sacked for corruption) running up and down the queue crying "Excellency?" ever more anxiously. Me? I wondered. But obviously not since he looked straight at me – short-hair, winter tan, fleece and jeans – and decided I wasn't ambassadorial material. Finally, a solid RMP corporal appeared, immediately distinguished me from anyone he would let within a mile of securing a toy-box and liberated me from the queue to head into town. My predecessor as ambassador still being around, I spent the next few days travelling the country incognito with a single bodyguard – an Australian ex-soldier called James, who was a great companion. It was the least encumbered I would be for the next two years.

A few weeks later, I arrived back as the ambassador for real this time. I soon settled into a routine with my new Close Protection team – six bodyguards and two Afghan drivers. Having thought this through, I set out the ground rules on Day 1, i.e. I would let them do their job and follow their advice, but I would never be photographed wearing body armour, since my job was to project confidence in our mission, and they were to risk shooting me if that were the only way to stop me being kidnapped, since I had no intention of ending my days in an orange jump-suit. Pete, my first team leader, swallowed hard but agreed. And so, on we went: up just before six for an hour in the gym, working breakfast, walk to the office and then the round of meetings, appointments and other engagements until late at night. Two cars, a smiling bodyguard ("BG" – everything in the military is abbreviated) sometimes in a suit if we needed to get him into a venue from which BGs were banned, advance teams to scope out the sites we visited and negotiate us through the endless checkpoints – Afghan much easier than American! – and drivers who could carve through the traffic without offending anyone. We had a tradition of getting out on a Friday morning (the Afghan weekend) for a hike or another activity, sometimes in preparation for a sponsored event for Help for Heroes. The other big tradition with every team was the team photo, usually taken after the arrival of the team polo shirts bearing the RMP logo, including one for me. Because this was at their expense, I decided to return the compliment, so got each of my teams first a British Embassy and then a NATO Afghanistan fleece or polo shirt. Spot the "ambo" in the photographs.

Within a few weeks, Pete's team was succeeded by Chris's, Chris by Ed, Ed by Lloyd, Lloyd by Jim and Jim by Richard. Team leaders were either grizzled veterans or enthusiastic adventurers. Their 2ICs were the same, but invariably the reverse, proving that, despite rumours to the contrary,

RMP Longmoor do have a plan. Each team had a youngster taking on huge responsibilities just as his school friends partied through their college days (although one or two managed to party through their embassy nights). Each team had the one who was not as fit as the rest and managed to avoid the gym or spend a little time on the cross-trainer. Each had the fit one, often also the one with an improbably all-over and orange suntan. There was usually the scally squaddie, who made everyone laugh, and most teams had an intense one, who leapt to his feet every time I wandered into the Ops Room and would relax only when talking about the bargain American (healthy!) muscle-building supplements he was stuffing into himself to make his civvie wardrobe obsolete so he could buy another pair of the latest 5.11 cargo pants.

As ambassador, you are never off duty and everyone wants a piece of you – except for one group, the CP team. They put their lives at risk to protect mine and understood without complaint that sometimes the robust approach I took to my job meant putting mine and thus theirs at greater risk than they should have had to accept. This was the group of guys who were with me 24/7, with whom I relaxed, joked, talked football and family. Many are now friends on Facebook and some will be friends for life.

Mark Sedwill, British Ambassador & NATO Representative Afghanistan (2010-11)

Quite often a special relationship develops between the Principal and the team with the responsibility bestowed upon the team not lost on the VIPs in their care. Regularly sharing adventures in some of the most dangerous areas, there is generally a joke or funny story to be shared and more often than not the Ambassador, High Commisioner or General feels as protective of his[8] team as they do of him. Without doubt the above accounts would be repeated by 99% (there have been the odd couple, who believed themselves invincible and beyond the need of the protection of a CP team) of the diplomats and military commanders, who have enjoyed the company of these small yet highly-professional teams.

Now may be a time for a brief mention of the other team members that are seldom acknowledged but offer a great deal of support to the teams,

---

8 For 'his' also read 'her' as many of the Ambassadors that have had the pleasure of the company of an RMP CP team have been women, Dame Maeve Fort, during her tenure as HMA in Beirut and Dame Rosalind Marsden, during her time as HMA in both Kabul and Khartoum to name but two.

namely, the animals that have been adopted along the way. In Kinshasa, a giant tortoise named 'Kinell' (in light of the response generally given by an individual on first seeing him) and was in excess of 100 years old, kept the team company(albeit slowly!) and in Khartoum, 'Georgie', the tortoise of regular proportions, would regularly munch through an operators forgotten flip- flop. The heroes though were the two team dogs in Beirut, who would go running with the members of the team and act as an eight-pawed CP team, snarling and growling at anyone whom they deemed suspicious – in fact anybody outside of the team. Tonto was a long-haired, Alsatian -Labrador cross and quite soft when you got to know him and Timmy was a Doberman crossed with a baseball bat, who would think nothing of seeing off anyone he didn't like and would regularly disappear for a few days before returning to the team covered in scrapes, bruises and invariably part of his ear missing. He once came home with shotgun pellets in his hind quarters that didn't seem to bother him at all. Luckily, the team had set up a Timmy Vet Fund so all his treatment was taken care of. Achilles was adopted by the SCR team in Afghanistan and had a penchant for eating anything at ear level. He later found a home with a wealthy businessman in Kabul when the team came home.

Such is the reputation of RMP Close Protection teams, a story entitled *'Protection Squad'* written by Mike Knowles with supporting artwork by Gordon Livingstone was published by Commando Comics in November 1993. The story followed the experiences of the fictional character LCpl Jack Johnson as he trained for and conducted Close Protection duties.

The synopsis of Commando 4245 Protection Squad read as follows:

Bored with paperwork and traffic duties, Lance-Corporal Jack Johnston of the Royal Military Police was on the lookout for excitement. So he volunteered for special duties and, after a spell of tough training, became a member of the elite Close Protection Squads. That was when he began to understand what real excitement was!

RMP CP enjoys a reputation as being the world leader in Close Protection, but although the RMP men and women, who have deployed in support of Close Protection operations are the epitome of professionalism, the FCO and those military commanders that benefit from this service are 'clients'

NATO Ambassador Mark Sedwill on an internal flight in Afghanistan travelling with a Political Advisor, Military Attaché and two bodyguards (out of shot).

and therefore a form of quality assurance must take place. This falls to the Officer Commanding or his designate and has been one of the core roles of the Command Team since the first deployments to Kampala and Beirut. Formally termed Pastoral Visits, Operational Evaluations, (OPEVAL), can last anything between a few days and a couple of weeks depending on the flights in and out of country and is an opportunity for the OC to visit the team, conduct an equipment audit and, most importantly, speak with the Principal to ensure he or she is receiving the service that they expect. These visits usually went without a hitch and the command team have enjoyed all that globetrotting can offer. However, as Lt Col (Retd) Ian Stenning MBE RMP, formally Officer Commanding of the RMP Ops Wing between 1992-1994, recalls it wasn't always plain sailing;

> Many of my fellow officers from outside the CP fraternity viewed my lifestyle with considerable envy. All I would say is that repeated trips up the A3 to LHR [London Heathrow Airport] and endless airports around the various continents was far from a sinecure. On one occasion, en route to Khartoum, we were diverted to Brussels when the pilot sadly suffered a fatal heart attack

at the helm. I then caught a flight up to Amsterdam for the next available seat to Khartoum. I had 24 hrs to kill in Amsterdam and caught the train from airport hotel to the centre of the city. On my return to the airport the train broke down and we sat in a carriage in mid-July temperatures for a couple of hours! I then got to Sudan to find the Embassy closed for the weekend, no local currency available and my hotel booking in jeopardy. Unbeknown to me at the time, this particular hotel was also home for the infamous terrorist Carlos the Jackal. However, sadly, I never had the pleasure of meeting him. Two days later, I came to leave Khartoum but my flights were delayed by about 10 hours. As we taxied to the runway, the oxygen masks all suddenly appeared but we were still on the ground! Instead of flying direct to Nairobi we went via Mogadishu and Addis Ababa and were not allowed off the aircraft, which was possibly good from a security perspective but not in relation to one's core temperature! I got to Nairobi and discovered that my holdall, which the Sudanese authorities had unusually insisted go in the aircraft hold, had been rifled and various items were missing. I then had a meaningful discussion with the airline staff in order to secure a seat on the last flight to Kampala. However, this flight was also not running to schedule and as I went to take my seat I was confronted with two frustrated passengers in the next row literally fighting over their seats! I eventually got to Kampala and

Tonto and Timmy, the CP Team's bodyguards in Beirut.

had an excellent visit, which included dinner with the High Commissioner and his family in the 7Hills restaurant on the edge of the city. The owner was aware of his VIP guests and had prepared elaborate place settings with far too many knives, forks, and spoons in an attempt to impress. The restaurant was also a disco and appeared to accommodate numerous young ladies of a professional disposition … ! I have kept my formal invite from the High Commissioner to what was a really most memorable occasion. Two days later, I was once again up early to catch a flight home but my departure was interrupted whilst I sought relief from my emergency supplies of Imodium; what else could go wrong!'

OPEVALS continue and can see Visiting Officers travelling to Algiers, Beirut, Kabul, Helmand and Columbia in a matter of weeks ensuring that the standing of the RMP CP teams remains at the pinnacle of this extremely competitive trade. Testament to the ongoing mission and continued relationship with the FCO, 31 years after the ECAB decision that lead to the RMP taking on responsibility for diplomatic protection abroad and 30 years after the first deployments to Kampala and Beirut, in June 2011 the staff of CPU was joined by the British Prime Minister, the Right Honorable David Cameron for a photograph on the steps of Number 10 Downing Street. Before the photograph was taken Mr. Cameron took a moment to thank the RMP for their professionalism and dedication to service in a very testing time for Her Majesty's Forces.

Chapter 6
Military Campaigns Post 1970

Close Protection in the military arena as we know it today can identify its foundations as being those laid within the conflicts of modern day including Aden, Malaya, Cyprus and Northern Ireland. But as those struggles faded away into memory, other conflicts emerged and continue to do so with uncomfortable regularity and with them the need for Close Protection continues.

The name and sovereignty of the Falkland Islands, South Georgia and the South Sandwich Islands in the South Atlantic Ocean east of Argentina have long been in dispute and, as a result of a protracted diplomatic confrontation between the United Kingdom and Argentina, the Falkland Conflict started on Friday 2 April 1982 with the Argentine invasion and occupation of the Falkland Islands and South Georgia. Britain launched a naval task force to engage the Argentine Navy and Argentine Air Force, in order to retake the islands by amphibious assault. The conflict ended with the Argentine surrender on 14 June 1982, and the islands remained under British control. The war lasted 74 days and resulted in the deaths of 257 British and 649 Argentine servicemen and 3 civilian Falkland islanders. It is the most recent external conflict to be fought by the UK without any allied states and the only external Argentine war since the 1880s. Interestingly, neither state officially declared war and the fighting was largely limited to the territories under dispute and the South Atlantic.

A number of RMP JNCOs deployed to the Falklands in support of close protection operations with Cpl 'Dixie' Dean RMP, attached to the Royal Marines and bodyguard to Major General Jeremy Moore, OBE, MC and Bar Commander British Land Forces; Cpl Malcolm Davies RMP (London District) and Cpl Tony Savage RMP (160 Pro Coy RMP, Aldershot) deployed as bodyguards to the Commander 5 Bde Brigadier Tony Wilson. On deployment, these NCOs came under the command of the Royal Marines and 5 Bde but following the surrender of the Argentine forces[1], Savage and Davies returned

---
1 Maj Gen Moore received the surrender of the Argentine commander, General de Brigada Mario Menéndez, in Port Stanley on 14 June 1982.

to General Police Duties under the watchful eye of Sgt Allan Barley RMP.

Before 1991, the RMP provided CP to the General Officer Commanding and Brigade Commanders of Northern Ireland. On 16 January 1991, following the invasion of Kuwait by Saddam Hussein's forces from Iraq, a coalition force that had assembled to counter the invasion started its offensive under the name Operation DESERT STORM. It was at this time that RMP CP was deployed to provide protection to our own military commanders including Lt General (later General) Sir Peter de la Billiere, a former CO of 22 SAS and the Commander of British Forces during the campaign. Bodyguards were also provided for the Brigade Commanders, not least Brigadier (later Major General) Patrick Cordingly, Commander of the 'Desert Rats'.

In 1999, with civil unrest in the Balkans, a team was established at very short notice to look after Major General FR Dannant CBE MC, Commander British Forces (COMBRITFOR), Kosovo. The following is a short article written by Sgt Chris Brice, that was published in The Royal Military Police Journal December 1999:

Close Protection to the Colonel Commandant

Then, all of a sudden, it was over. We were both back in Longmoor awaiting the debrief. The team, Corporals Chris Brice and Colin Harker, had just returned from Pristina, Kosovo after 7 whole weeks (long enough for a medal) providing protection for Major General FR Dannatt CBE MC, Commander British Forces (COMBRITFOR).

It had all begun one stormy Saturday night when the phone rang. The disguised voice at the other end seemed to be inviting us for a holiday in the Balkans, at a venue to be decided. Normal brown and green holiday attire was to be worn, as we were to look after the Colonel Commandant RMP. Fantastic! A General to look after must mean the finest hotels that Macedonia and Kosovo could offer. How wrong we were. The only hotels that we saw were green and canvas.

Still, our first stop was Longmoor for a 40 minute PDT, with just enough time to zero and test fire our weapons, before flying straight out to Skopje, Macedonia. Once there and having met the General, we tried to introduce the Division to the delights of working with a CP team – not as easy as it sounds. There were many difficulties from the outset, but once it was realised that there was reasoning behind the requests, the Division and its staff accepted us.

After a short stint in Macedonia, during which we managed to see all of the units preparing to move into Kosovo, it was time for them to move north and head for Pristina. On the day of the big push, it was awesome to watch British troops crossing through the Kacanik Defile with Union Flags flying from antennae, provoking that sentiment they call patriotism. We followed shortly afterwards by road and if it hadn't been for a RMP motorcyclist and his traffic control abilities, we would've been late for the ball.

Once we reached Pristina, the main threat was from the remaining VJ troops [Yugoslav Army] and sympathisers. The amount of press and media within the Province's capital was vast. The 'Boss' in his capacity as COMBRITFOR, was responsible initially for safeguarding Britain's interests, which entailed numerous high profile interviews with the international media. The early days in Pristina were the most exciting. Throughout the tour, the Boss was a true gent and the ADC was good for morale. The team comprised of the General's driver, the General's signaller and us. For the two non-RMP, the learning curve was mountainous! To their credit they came through with shining colours.

Seven weeks down the line, we had accomplished the mission. We had visited two countries, met a member of the Royal Family, two Cabinet Ministers, flown in all of KFOR's helicopters and were even included in the RMP Kosovo photograph. Who said life was dull?

A CP Team was also deployed to Bosnia, responsible for the safety of the Rt. Hon. Lord Ashdown, who had been appointed as the High Representative of Bosnia and Herzegovina based in Sarajevo between May 2002 and May 2006. On 14th March 2002, Lord Ashdown testified as witness for the prosecution at the trial of Slobodan Milošević[2], who had been indicted for war crimes, making Lord Ashdown a highly prominent target for those supporters of Milošević. In 2003, Sgt (later WO2) 'Shep' Shephard was deployed to Bosnia with his team looking after Lord Ashdown. On 20th September 2003, former US President, Bill Clinton flew into Bosnia to formally open the Srebrenica Genocide Memorial, recognising the 8,000 Bosnian males of fighting age,

---

2 Slobodan Milošević; (20 August 1941 – 11 March 2006) was President of Serbia and of Yugoslavia. He served as the President of Socialist Republic of Serbia and Republic of Serbia from 1989 until 1997 in three terms and as President of the Federal Republic of Yugoslavia from 1997 to 2000. He also led the Socialist Party of Serbia from its foundation in 1990. In the midst of NATO bombings of Serbia, Milošević was charged with crimes against humanity by the International Criminal Tribunal for the former Yugoslavia (ICTY), but the trial ended after Milošević died in his cell.

who were executed by Serbian forces in July 1995. Having served in Bosnia in 1995 and 1996, Sgt Shephard was appointed bodyguard to Lord Ashdown for the day and together they flew in with Clinton, the rest of the team securing the area in advance. When on the ground, Sgt Sheppard remembers Lord Ashdown asking him and his Team Leader, SSgt Stuart 'Dutch' Holland, how many bodyguards Bill Clinton had, to which Sgt Shephard replied "about 30 odd". Lord Ashdown then asked how many bodyguards he himself had. "Four!" replied SSgt Holland, "and one of those is probably sat in the car down the road reading a book!"

The War in Afghanistan began on October 7th, 2001, with the US military's Operation ENDURING FREEDOM, that was launched, along with the British military, in response to the September 11, 2001 attacks on the US. The UK has, since 2002, led its own military operation, Operation HERRICK, as part of the same war in Afghanistan. The character of the war evolved from a violent struggle against Al-Qaeda and its Taliban supporters to a complex counter-insurgency effort.

The first phase of the war was the aftermath of the attacks of September 11, 2001, when the United States launched Operation Enduring Freedom, to remove the safe haven to Al-Qaeda and its use of the Afghan territory as a base of operations for terrorist activities. In that first phase, U.S. and coalition forces, working with the Afghan opposition forces of the Northern Alliance, quickly ousted the Taliban regime. During the following Karzai administration, the character of the war shifted to an effort aimed at smothering an insurgency hostile to the US-backed Karzai government, in which the insurgents preferred not to directly confront the International Security Assistance Force (ISAF) troops, but blended into the local population and mainly used Improvised Explosive Devices (IEDs) and suicide bombings.

The stated aim of the invasion was to find Osama bin Laden and other high-ranking Al-Qaeda members to be put on trial, to destroy the organization of Al-Qaeda, and to remove the Taliban regime, which supported and gave safe haven to it. The Bush administration stated that, as policy, it would not distinguish between terrorist organizations and nations or governments that harboured them.

ISAF had been established by the UN Security Council at the end of December 2001 to secure Kabul and the surrounding areas. NATO assumed control of ISAF in 2003. By July 23, 2009, ISAF had around 64,500 troops from 42 countries, with NATO members providing the core of the force. The

NATO commitment is important, because it demonstrates that this is a global effort aimed at tackling a global problem in international terrorism. According to ISAF Key Facts and Figures dated 1st December 2013, the United States still had 60,000 troops supporting the mission in Afghanistan.

Throughout the enduring campaign, RMP have provided Close Protection teams to the British Ambassador, Deputy Commander ISAF, two other command appointments based in Kabul as well as the Regional Commander and Brigade Commander based in Kandahar and Helmand provinces respectively in the south of the country. WO2 Wayne Owen RMP led a team working for Maj Gen Nick Carter[3] CBE DSO, Regional Commander South based in Kandahar, which led to very interesting patrols around the city as well as joint patrols with US forces. In such high- threat environments, CP teams cannot operate alone and will deploy on the ground with support from soldiers from the local battle group. Cpl Ben Slater RMP, whilst on CP duties with Brig (later Maj Gen) John Lorimer, Task Force Helmand Commander, the team was supported by the Special Forces Support Group.

The nature of the threat presented by the conflicts in both Iraq and Afghanistan has seen a massive development of kit and equipment available to teams. With bodyguards operating on the ground with soldiers from the battle group, the covert approach is in the most part forgotten, with teams having a requirement to operate fully overtly. The latest body armour with load carrying capacity is now issued, along with C8 rifles fitted with grenade launchers, high explosive grenades, distraction grenades, Light Machine Gun, satellite communication, GPS and purpose-built armoured Toyota Land Cruisers (a far cry from the Jeeps of 1954!). With the continued threat of an IED attack, travel in helicopters is commonplace but if none are available, Principals would often travel in fully armoured military vehicles such as the Mastiff or join coalition partners in their own vehicles such as the Stryker APC.

In January 2003, the Defence Secretary, Mr. Geoffrey Hoon, announced that 45,000 service personnel including 26,000 from Land Forces were to deploy to Iraq and the call went out for CP operators to attend Longmoor for Pre Deployment Training as soon as possible. As a result, Longmoor saw the largest gathering of operators in its history with Building 30 being the focal point. In all, 45 CP trained personnel arrived at Longmoor, some from existing deployments, (Sgt (later SSgt) Woodward was busy protecting the

---

3   Later promoted to Lt General and Deputy Commandant of the RMP.

Brigade Commander in Banja Luka when he got the call) and some who were regarded as very seasoned and believed their CP career was well and truly behind them were called to task. Teams were allocated to various commanders in Bahrain, Jordon, Kuwait, Jakarta, Ryhad, Jeddah and latterly Baghdad. The pre deployment training was fast and furious and some operators, who had not deployed for a number of years bought some very 'interesting' ideas and drills to the table. Ultimately, all teams deployed saw their principals safely through the war. On cessation of hostilities a number of teams joined forces in Baghdad with the remaining returning home.

RMP continued to offer CP to the Ambassador and theatre-based commanders both in Baghdad and Basra. In 2006, SSgt Keightley RMP (as Team Leader), Sgt Karl Shone RMP, Sgt Paul Andrews RM, Cpl 'Taff' Clark RMP, Cpl Nathan Chapman RMP and Cpl 'Simmo' Simpson RLC deployed to Baghdad as the Close Protection Team for Lt General Sir Rob Fry KCB CBE RM, the Deputy Commander General of the coalition forces. The tour was frantic from beginning to end with insurgent activity in the city and outer regions a constant threat. SSgt Keightley and Cpl Chapman escorted the General on a trip to Ramadi, which was a hotbed of fighting between insurgents and the US marines stationed in the town. After landing in a Black Hawk helicopter, the Marines drove the VIP party through the town to the Governor's office, (narrowly missing a suicide bomb attack), which was in a two storey building in the centre of the town. The Governor's office was situated on the ground floor with a US Marine look out post on the first. The meeting with the Governor commenced with both SSgt Keightley and Cpl Chapman in the office looking on, the Marines providing the outer cordon. Shortly after the meeting started, it was as if all hell had broken loose outside with the Americans on the first floor engaging with .50 calibre machine gun and grenades with small arms fire incoming. The noise was quite deafening in the office and, reminiscent of the scene in the film 'Carry on up the Khyber', dust was falling from the ceiling and there were a few anxious faces. The gun battle continued, but the General, being a very calm collected, individual, simply leaned forward and said to the Governor "Would you mind speaking up?" To top it all, a US Marine Sgt approached the CP Team Leader and explained that there was an enemy sniper embedded in the building opposite and that if the General wanted to return to Baghdad, he would have to leave at that moment, into the line of fire, and into the vehicles! In addition, it transpired that an insurgent regularly engaged the call-signs as they left the building with

MILITARY CAMPAIGNS POST 1970   163

Pictured by their Stryker APC: Maj General Carter (centre facing – later Lt General and Commander Land Forces) and his Team Leader, WO2 Wayne Owen RMP (far right).

Cpl Ben Slater mounted in a weapon mounted installation kit (WMIK) Land Rover during his tenure as bodyguard to Brigadier John Lorimer, Task Force Helmand Commander in Afghanistan, 2007.

Cpl Ben Slater RMP with Brig Lorimer (second from right) whilst in Helmand Province, Afghanistan. Cpl Slater can be seen carrying his C8 rifle with Underslung Grenade Launcher (UGL) fitted.

WO2 Wayne Owen RMP awaiting uplift by an RAF Chinook.

an RPG and it was the Team Leader's job to engage him if he appeared. The movement of a principal into a known hostile environment goes completely against the grain in the world of Close Protection, but the General wanted to leave on time and that is what happened. Thankfully, the sniper turned out to be a poor shot when under fire and the insurgent with the RPG failed to appear. All was good and the General continued on his trip and his return to Baghdad. Since Operation Desert Storm, RMP CP Teams have deployed in every military campaign since.

Royal Military Police Close Protection, whether in support of the Government or Military, offers soldiers opportunities they would not experience and relationships with high-ranking Military Commanders and Ambassadors they would not normally spend five minutes with in regular service let alone six month tours. The bond between Principal and team is one of mutual trust and respect and, on occasions, a SSgt Team Leader will inform a 3 or 4 star General that his proposed programme is neither safe or sensible. There may be some grumblings but the opinion of the team is respected and the 'Boss' will listen to the advice given.

Chapter 7

Joint Operations

Before the RMP were appointed by the British Government, 22 SAS were deployed to high-risk theatres, in order to provide protection to at-risk VIPs. As the global threat of terrorism grew steadily worse, the SAS were tasked to fulfil other duties and could not commit fully to the close protection mission. The RMP took over and in the early days the SAS would establish the mission before handing over to the RMP team, who would have had the time to form up and prepare at Longmoor before deploying, allowing the SAS to return to UK. Eventually the CP commitment fell solely on the RMP. Between 1994 and 1995, Lt Gen Sir Michael Rose KCB, CBE, DSO, QGM was appointed as Commander United Nations Protection Force in Bosnia (formerly Yugoslavia).

The conflict in Yugoslavia was as a result of tensions that had been bubbling away for a number of years between (mostly) Serbians and Croats. In 1990, following political wrangling by the Serb, Slobodan Milošević, head of the League of Communists of Serbia, the tensions developed into all-out civil war, resulting in the worst war crimes that Europe had witnessed since World War II.

Lt Gen Rose had seen service in the Middle East, Aden, Malaysia, Northern Ireland and Dhofar. As the Commander of the UN mission, (Commander United Nations Protection Force – COMDUNPROFOR), Rose was to deploy with a Close Protection team to ensure his personal security. Following direction by the MOD in Whitehall, a Close Protection team consisting of BRITCON UNPROFOR and RMP were deployed with the General, including SSgt Frank Cannon RMP and after 6 months in, SSgt Clive Davies RMP.

After 12 months, Lt Gen Rose was succeeded by Lt Gen Rupert Smith and the combination of a joint team configuration continued. This team consisted 2 members of the BRITCON CP assets, 2 US forces signalers and SSgt Jim Sorbie. Again the teams changed over at the six month point and, in addition to the US Special Forces soldiers, the US support continued in the form of 'Flashbang' and 'Det Cord' and SSgt 'Taff' Pike RMP(who later went on to become the Operations Officer at CPU). The following is an account of one of his 'fond' memories of that operation that typifies the sense of humour inherent with the British squaddie:

> The role was to provide CP to COMUNPROFOR, Lt Gen Rupert Smith. On 24 July 1995, Ratko Mladic[1], the then Commander of the Main Staff of the VRS or Army of Repulika Srpska (Bosnian-Serb Army) was indicted by the International Criminal Tribunal for the former Yugoslavia (ICTY), accused of genocide, crimes against humanity and various war crimes.
>
> Notwithstanding this, he remained in power so COMUNPROFOR was forced to engage with him on a fairly regular basis.
>
> On one such occasion, we attended the Bosnian-Muslim enclave of Zepa, which was falling into Serb hands. This followed very closely after the fall of Srebrenica, where thousands of Bosniak males were murdered by Serbian troops, allegedly on Mladic's orders. During something of a surreal day, upon arrival at Zepa, Smith had a 'tense' meeting with Mladic, during which it appeared that Mladic attempted to get Smith to 'raise a toast'. However, the covert camera crew, operating from inside a tent, were spotted by the CP team and with Smith alerted to their presence, any potential embarrassment was diffused.
>
> We then moved to a hillside overlooking Zepa and, surrounded by Mladic's henchmen, watched as the town was liberated or ethnically cleansed, depending on which side of the fence you sit. From my own perspective, and I know there are arguments over exactly what happened, all I can say is that I watched a town start to burn from end to end. Shots rang out but it was impossible to say from our viewing point who was shooting at whom or what. There were two theories from that day about the burning of the town. The first is that it was the Serbs burning the town down; the second, that it was the Bosniaks burning their own homes rather than see them occupied by the Serbs.
>
> The surrealism continued as we left the hill and attended a BBQ hosted by Mladic.
>
> On another occasion, a meeting had been arranged between Smith and Mladic near Banja Luka at a lakeside lodge, the name of which I do not recall. The party consisted of Smith, his MA, Lt Col Baxter, Ginge, Chris, myself and one US signaler. At that time, flights in and out of Sarajevo had

---

1 Ratko Mladic was accused of masterminding appalling acts of violence against Muslims during the Bosnian conflict and was finally arrested on 26 May, 2011, after 16 years in hiding.

been suspended due to the security situation but on this occasion authority had been given by Mladic for Smith and team to make a helicopter flight to attend the meeting. A bright white, UN marked, Westland Sea King, flown by Royal Navy pilots out of Split made the flight to Sarajevo where we embarked. However, within seconds of taking off and clearing the airport perimeter fence, several loud bangs were heard and vibrations felt throughout the aircraft. Despite Maldic's assurances, we had been engaged by a rogue member of the Bosnian-Serb Army, who had peppered the underneath of the helicopter resulting in several holes in the fuel tanks. Whilst not catastrophic, this forced the aircraft to divert to Kiseljak, where the damage and flow of spilling fuel could be clearly seen. More phone calls ensued, which allegedly resulted in Mladic 'promising to have the culprit killed'.

The result was that, with new assurances in place, a replacement Sea King transported us to Banja Luka. Our lumbering helicopter landed way behind Bosnian-Serb lines in a field alongside the lodge and it was immediately apparent that there was a very heavy Bosnian-Serb Army presence securing the HLS. The party disembarked and the meeting took place. On its completion, Smith and Mladic walked back to the aircraft. Ginge, Chris and myself were on the ground and the signaler was on board. We all carried personal radios, each with an earpiece. Remembering that Mladic had been indicted by the ICTY, over my radio I received a message from Ginge stating that, "We're going to grab Mladic". I remember looking at the plethora of Bosnian-Serb troops surrounding us, the dormant Sea King that had already proved vulnerable that day and then across at Chris, who just shrugged his shoulders. With that, the rotors started to turn and Ginge's voice came through my earpiece again, "When he gets close to the cargo door, we're going to bundle him on". Another nonchalant shrug from Chris and I remember thinking, "This is mental. There is no way that this will get off the ground if we grab Mladic" and, facing out [CP operators never look in], started picking targets in my arcs of fire. Ginge's voice again, "As soon as he gets close to the door". Pause. "Standby, standby" By now the rotors were fully revved up and the sound was quite deafening but I clearly heard Ginge say, "Standby … … .Standby … … … ..Whaaaaaaaaaa". W*****! I often wonder how history would read if we'd misheard him and started shooting.

Capt 'Taff' Pike RMP

Following the signing of the Dayton Agreement[2] in December 1995, control of the mission in the Balkans was passed from the United Nations to NATO and a CP team consisting of 4 members of the RMP continued to support operations and provided protection for Commander Allied Rapid Reaction Corps (COM ARRC)[3], Gen Sir Michael Walker KCB CMG CBE ADC Gen.

With the agreement signed, more VVIPs and VIPs were able to visit the region and subsequently a specialist close protection section was formed. The Joint Visitors Bureau (JVB) Close Protection Team consisted of 7 RMP CP operators and 3 drivers from the Royal Logistic Corps. Visitors who benefited from the team's protection included His Royal Highness, the Prince of Wales, John Major (then Prime Minister) and Paddy Ashdown GCMG, KBE (who later became the High Representative for Bosnia and Herzegovina with his own RMP CP team).

Cpl (later SSgt) 'Flash' Hannan RMP was a member of the team and was tasked with protecting Field Marshal Sir Peter Inge. During the visit programme, the Field Marshal was to drive to Sarajevo from the HQ compound in Llizda in order to witness for himself the damage that had been caused during the war. The convoy consisted of four vehicles and the serial was to take approximately an hour. On leaving the confines of the camp, Field Marshal Inge ordered the Team Leader to stop the convoy as he had seen that two Army Air Corps Lynx helicopters were on the pan and that he would like to fly to the next serial not drive. As there had been no pre-arrangement, the Team Leader explained that it might take some time to arrange, to which the Field Marshal replied "Sort it out". The task fell upon the BG and the subsequent conversation between him and the air crew is reported as follows:

BG: "Hey can I speak to someone in charge please"
AAC Sgt: "What's up mate?"
BG: "I need to arrange a City flight right now for my boss".
AAC Sgt: "Ha ha! No chance we were all on the p*** last night."

---

2   The General Framework Agreement for Peace in Bosnia and Herzegovina, also known as the Dayton Agreement is the peace agreement reached at Wright-Patterson Air Force Base near Dayton, Ohio in November 1995. The agreement was formally signed in Paris on 14 December 1995 and put an end to the three and a half year long war in Bosnia.
3   ARRC is the British led High Readiness Multinational NATO operational capability whose motto is 'Fortune, favours the brave'. The purpose of ARRC is to deploy operationally in support of NATO and the EU in order to support crisis management options or to sustain current operations.

BG: "I am not being funny, I need to sort this out. Can I speak to your OC?"
Enter AAC officer: "What is going on?"
BG: "Sir, I need to sort a City flight out right now for my boss, he's waiting outside."
Officer: "Who the f*** are you?"
BG: "I am Cpl Hannan of the JVB Close Protection Team."
Officer: "I don't give a s***. I have grounded all aircraft today, no-one is flying anywhere!"
BG: "Oh, ok sir, I'll just tell the boss, he may want to come in and speak to you."
Officer: "I couldn't care less … . Who is your boss?"
BG: "Field Marshal Sir Peter Inge and he is waiting in the car outside."

After a brief career-changing period of decision-making, the officer had his staff running around in a highly efficient manner and the BG before leaving calmly asked, "Shall I tell him the flight is on then Sir?"

In March 1997 as a result of the collapse of the financial system in Albania, alleged fraud during elections and economic crises, the government led by President Sali Ram Berisha collapsed and was stripped of all legitimacy in 1997. A period of civil unrest followed that led to a European Union military mission led by Italy being sent to stabalise the country.

At the time, the United Kingdom had a diplomatic mission based in Albania's capital, Tirana, and it was decided, in light of the increased threat of violence, that they would require protection. The Foreign and Commonwealth Office made a formal request to the Ministry of Defence, out of which two military operations were formulated. OP PENNY whose mandate was the protection of Her Majesty's Ambassador, Andrew Tesoriere, and OP HAVEN with the mission of providing protection to other British nationals inside the country. The RMP were mobilized to undertake theses taskings with SSgt 'Taff' Pike charged to lead on OP PENNY.

With the mission given the go-ahead, all kit and equipment was packed and sealed at Longmoor and, within 18 hours, SSgt Pike was at Heathrow airport meeting with other CP assets awaiting a flight to Tirana via Rome.

By the time the team reached Rome, the situation in Tirana had deteriorated and the airport had been closed, which denied the team access by normal means and an alternative method of entry was required. An RAF HS125 jet was diverted off task and the team was then flown to Gioia Del Colle airbase,

C8 5.56mm rifle: Length 750mm – Weight 2.7kg – Muzzle velocity 280 m/s – Rate of fire 700-900rpm – Effective range 260m.

where the RAF had permanent assets. SSgt Pike, who in addition to his own kit was responsible for some extremely cumbersome communications destruction kit, then assembled his insertion plan. He secured two MoD Land Rovers which were then moved tactically to the compound of the Embassy of the United States in Tirana. They were then moved across to the British Embassy.

Other than a British Embassy vehicle being stolen, sporadic gunfire and low level criminality, there was no directed threat against British personnel and, except for a 'rescue' of the inhabitants from a UK-run orphanage, the tour was relatively uneventful.

Although planned operations with other Brigade CP assets have for the time being ceased, the relationship between RMP CP and them continues with teams co-located within certain posts allowing for the exchange of information and intelligence. There have been odd instances when a team has been embroiled with an ongoing Brigade CP assets mission due to the appointment of the Principal and their desire to be in the thick of it. The following is an account by Sgt Andy Heron RMP, whose team provided support to what began as an Afghan Army-led operation , whilst serving within Helmand Province, Afghanistan.

Close Protection Team Leader Task Force Helmand (TFH) OP HERRICK

Friday 29 Jan 2010, in the run-up to OP MOSHTERAK, Taliban fighters attacked the Bost Hotel in Lashkar Gah, the capital of Helmand Province.

About 1000hrs local time, militants took over an empty four-storey building under construction near the Afghan Shaewali Bks and Provincial

Governors compound and opened fire on soldiers and police.

Word reached TFH HQ of the attack and immediately the QRF [Quick Reaction Force] from the Grenadier Guards were on stand-by in their Panther armoured vehicles to make the 10 minute drive to the Governors road. The CP Team were stood up to deploy with the Bde Comd and it was a case of find a seat in the vehicle and off you went.

Afghan forces were making every attempt to re-claim the building but were taking casualties. A number of British troops were now on site and on hand to help if needed. The Bde Comd wanted to get closer to the building to make an assessment, so along with his CP Team that's what he did. With the fire-fight still in full swing the team moved across open ground and into the ground floor of the building. Making the best of a bad situation as a clearance was being carried out, the Comd moved on and up the floors, with glass falling down as rooms were being cleared and, with a steady rate of fire, the fire fight continued. Afghan forces began to take the upper hand. The QRF vehicles, which were parked some 100m away towards the Governors compound, were the source of an ammo re-supply and someone needed to make the journey across 'no man's land' to bring the ammo to the fight, a job taken by the CP Team. A short time after leaving the hotel, Cpl Crofts RMP (V) returned with ammo, out of breath and half covered in sewage having fallen in a drain on his way – much to the amusement of the Comd and the team!

Eventually the building was re-taken. The whole day highlighted how much as a CP Team you can find yourself in any environment, one minute Algiers the next Helmand[4].

---

4   For further details of this incident visit: http://www.youtube.com/watch?v=1jvJwqm FEYA&feature=youtube_gdata_player

Chapter 8
Close Protection Unit Royal Military Police

Over the years it became apparent that more cohesion was required between the Operational and Training elements of RMP CP and in 1996 under the Command of Major (later Colonel) Jeremy Green RMP, who was the OC of the Ops Wing, both wings became what is now the Close Protection Unit Royal Military Police (CPU RMP). On 1st December 2004, Kitchener House (below) was officially opened by PM (A) Brig Colin Findlay MBE (himself attending the CP course in 1982), and the CPU united under one roof at last.

In addition to the training and subsequent deployment of individuals and teams, the CPU RMP also provides specialist training to foreign drivers, who are employed by the FCO in missions abroad, and military drivers who deploy with RMP CP teams as well as Close Quarter Combat and Team Medic

Kitchener House.

The Rt Hon Bob Ainsworth MP being briefed by SSgt Richard Keightley before being put through his paces by a CPU instructor. (Photographs taken by Cpl Ben Ross, CPU and reproduced with the kind permission of the Office of the Rt Hon Bob Ainsworth MP, Coventry North East.)

CLOSE PROTECTION UNIT ROYAL MILITARY POLICE

CPU Reunion 2012 with General Richards seated centre to the right (facing) of the OC CPU, Maj Mark John (wearing dark rugby shirt).

courses. Close relations are also held with civilian police counterparts and training teams are deployed abroad to instruct Close Protection and counter terrorist operations to those agencies that request it (with the blessing of the Permanent Joint Headquarters!). Understandably, the CPU had regular visits from military commanders and members of Parliament. On 28th August 2008, the Rt Hon Bob Ainsworth, Armed Forces Minister visited and along with the presentation of some medals to members of CPU, he was also shown around and put through his paces on the Urban Training Complex.

In 2012, the Close Protection Unit held a reunion that saw members of the RMP CP family past and present join together once again and, such is its reputation, the Chief of the Defence Staff, General Sir David Richards, GCB, CBE, DSO, attended having enjoyed the company of Royal Military Police Close Protection Teams for much of his career.

Chapter 9
Training Today

CPU RMP now conducts four eight week CP courses a year with spaces for 30 students on each. Places are available to all three service police formations as well as foreign students and, to date, these have included candidates from Australia, Kuwait, Lebanon, Pakistan, UAE, Canada, Norway, New Zealand and Saudi Arabia. Much like the foundation courses of 1961 and 1975 respectively, the CP course today has a focus on physical training, ranges and driving. There is also much emphasis on protocol and the ability to communicate at all command levels. Tactical Driving forms a great deal of the programme and is introduced early on in the course with the instructors having attended the Civil Police Advanced Driving Courses with Greater Manchester Police, Lancashire Constabulary or Hampshire Constabulary.

The course starts on the Sunday evening with what is known as 'ice breakers', which allow all the students to introduce themselves and tell a little about their lives so far. Following that, equipment is issued and the programme explained. Then after supper in Chateau Maurice, (named after the former Head Chef at the CPU mess), it is an hour or so of preparation for the following day before bed. Depending on the time of year, it is up at 0600 for PT and the course truly begins. The following short piece has been written by Cpl Mick Collier and LCpl Drew Bowness, who passed the Close Protection Course in 2010 and found themselves deployed on CP operations in Afghanistan soon after.

> Attending the Close Protection course at Longmoor in January 2010 proved to be one of the most challenging eight weeks of our careers. The training lived up to its reputation for exacting standards through a regime designed to test fully all aspects of our mental and physical stamina.
>
> The build-up for the course differed between us as LCpl Bowness had to participate in a Pre-Selection Course held at his unit, designed to see if candidates were suitable for the course and up to the required standard. Cpl Mick Collier was on exercise when he received a phone call asking if he would be interested in attending the Close Protection Course with a view to protecting 16 Air Assault Brigade Commander on Op Herrick 13 should he

be successful.

Having been briefed beforehand about the rigours of the timetable and the comparatively low success rates achieved in the past, we were both full of trepidation about the challenge ahead. However, when we arrived at Longmoor on Sunday 10th January 2010, we were both determined to pass, joining another 13 students with the same thoughts in mind.

As expected, the programme was full-on and did not allow an opportunity to sit still for one minute. As the course progressed, some students sustained minor injuries and were returned to their units to recover and some did not meet the necessary criteria and the reduction in numbers led to a bond forming between the surviving candidates. This served to sharpen our focus towards our goal and increased still further our determination to complete the course.

The training on the course, which all students had to pass, included C8 Diemarco rifle and Sig Sauer P229 pistol training, PT, tactical driving, Protocol, anti-ambush training, Close Quarter Combat, Rural and Urban walking drills. Many days were spent on the 'Pit Range' honing shooting skills and practicing drawing from the holster. The pistol shooting culminated in the Individual Bodyguard assessment, which entailed the student saving a VIP (in this case a dummy weighing 75kg) and extracting 'him' from the kill zone whilst firing at targets.

All of these skills could be called upon and used on an operational tour by a CP operator. Although the training schedule was designed with an emphasis toward measuring physical attributes and marksmanship skills, personal presentation and controlled behaviour was measured throughout.

One of the most daunting challenges for us both was the stretcher race, which is an important element of the programme as it is designed to encourage team work under pressure. The 'stretcher' is made up of two railway sleepers held together with scaffold poles and weighs approximately 100kg. The route is heinous and very challenging as within the first mile your team is taken through a swamp. Coupled with the weight of the stretcher the swamp (though not that deep, feels as though it is trying to swallow you). For 6 miles it was a real "Man Test" but, upon completion, there was a real sense of achievement; a weight lifted from our shoulders, in more ways than one.

The course culminated in a meticulously-planned exercise in conjunction with the civilian police. Exercise Watchtower was designed to test the

The final push of the 6 mile stretcher race up 'Heartbreak' hill and to the finish. (Cpl Steve Gray, wearing No 10, went on to become an instructor at the Close Protection Unit.)

students in all they had learnt over the previous seven weeks.

At this stage, the students have one last week to push; the most challenging so far. The subject VIP was picked up at an airport and afforded 24-hour protection across a series of events which included a visit to the inner quarters of 10 Downing Street, Chequers, the London Eye and other various locations across the south of England. Watchtower is a unique exercise, different from any other in the British Military and it often presented some very surreal moments.

The highlight of the exercise was when the VIP convoy was travelling along the A272. A marked police vehicle performed a twelve car overtake to get in front of our convoy, stopped our vehicles to inform the bodyguard there was an ambush in place a mile down the road. Out of the blue, two British Army Lynx Helicopters landed on the road in front of the vehicles and the Principal and Bodyguard made their extraction by air leaving the rest of the team to return by road.

The training at Longmoor has provided a firm foundation from which to develop our skills and has fully prepared us for our first close protection deployment to Afghanistan only a few weeks following completion of the course. Our principal was the NATO Senior Civilian Representative to

TRAINING TODAY 179

Ex LCpl Drew Bowness (right) changing magazines during one of the attacks on Exercise Watchtower.

A CPU Instructor, lying in wait as one of the 'enemy' in the back of a dumper truck on Exercise Watchtower.

Confronting the ambush somewhere in the Sussex Countryside.

Afghanistan, Mark Sedwill, a Four Star appointment. We now look forward to the next CP tour.

To ensure the effectiveness of the training, all instructors would have deployed on CP operations and senior instructors would have been Team Leaders. The eight weeks training culminates in Exercise Watchtower, which is held over a week all over the south of England and enables teaching staff to evaluate the students prior to receiving the all-important pass certificate. Public as well as Military venues are used and the assistance of outside agencies are paramount towards the success of the exercise.

On successful completion of the course, students will be invited back to Longmoor to attend pre-deployment training, where they will join other team members, conduct four weeks theatre-specific training before departing to one of the many hotspots in which RMP CP teams operate.

CPU still conducts the FCO driving course, over thirty years since its inception, and lends its expertise in the field of Close Protection to many different nations around the world.

CPU has on a regular basis provided training and support for different nations all over the world and this can be as little as offering advice to conducting fully-blown Close Protection courses. In 2005, a small advisory

TRAINING TODAY 181

Ex SSgt 'Flash' Hannan and Ex SSgt Mal Scott training for deployment on N2 at Longmoor. (Photograph reproduced with kind permission of Headquarters Recruiting Group Army Recruiting Team.)

team visited Israel and the following account taken from the August 2005 *RMP Corps Journal* shows how diverse life can be within the world of CP, whilst offering unique opportunities:

> Between the 14th and the 18th of March 2005, the Officer Commanding, Major Pat Cairns and Operations Warrant Officer, Mick Lycett were tasked on a CP advisory visit to Israel to look at the protective measures surrounding the new Palestinian President, Mahmoud Abbas (aka Abu mazen). Rumour has it the task was generated directly from No. 10 Downing Street following the Palestinian Conference in London, early March.
>
> Whilst both members of the Short Term Training Team (STTT) were based in Tel Aviv, the week was spent travelling the Palestinian strongholds of the West Bank and Gaza Strip, which, as those lucky enough to have made the trip will tell, it is no mean feat negotiating the Israeli Security Force checkpoints.
>
> However, on the 'other side', our hosts were more than hospitable and keen to show us their skill in the art of Close Protection. What became very apparent was their lack of reasonably serviceable equipment, from firearms

From the purpose-built ranges of Longmoor CP operators must find areas to train when deployed. These ranges can often be littered with debris, empty cases and children collecting the brass. The one that Capt (Ret'd) Devenney RMP is using above, is a military range in Afghanistan with the differences between this and one you would find in the UK obviously apparent.

to vehicles. However, it was explained that a great deal had been destroyed over the years with clashes with Israeli security forces.

The Palestinians are a proud race, no doubt through their training and hard-gained experience. But they were not afraid to give to us a seemingly never-ending shopping list, from armoured vehicles to ECM, to hand to Mr Blair and his government.

The highlights of the trip must fall to the guided tour of the Ramallah Compound, the widely publicised home of former President, Yasser Arafat. The Second-in-Command of the President's Special Guard, PLO Colonel Moneer Alzoabi spared nothing in his hospitality, even showing us Arafat's private quarters, which reputedly have been sealed since his death, and kindly allowing us to take a few photographs inside his private shrine.

CPU is a very fortunate organisation, which has the opportunity to visit

TRAINING TODAY 183

By contrast, this CP operator can be seen with an HK
MP5 on a 'range' near Sarajevo in 2005.

places few get to see. Even in these circumstances, this advisory visit must
be deemed quite extraordinary. Who knows where it will lead in the future?

Chapter 10
The 'Protegimus'

It would seem that, since its inception, the 'Protegimus' logo has been synonymous with RMP Close Protection operations around the world. The design for the original logo came from the hand of Ex Sgt 'Punchy' Pete Glover some 36 years ago. Whilst serving with 177 Pro Coy in Northern Ireland in 1974 it became apparent that unit logos and mottos were becoming very popular to symbolise the role which that particular unit was undertaking. Sgt Glover approached his OC, Capt John Allwood, and suggested that 177 should follow suit and that he would take on the task. Firstly came the idea of the motto, 'We Protect'. A simple yet apt description of what the unit represented. Sgt Glover believed that a Latin or Greek spin on the motto would give it more impact and following a conversation with the secretary of the Army Catholic Padre followed by a couple of hours waiting, the secretary passed a piece of grubby notepaper to Sgt Clover on which was written 'Haec PROTEGIMUS'. The secretary assured Sgt Glover that this was a literal translation of 'We Protect' and that the meaning of 'Haec' was translated as 'this' and did not need to be included. Now having a motto; a motif was required. Sgt Glover drew from his memory of visiting the armouries of the Tower of London as a child and designed the knight's helmet and breastplate that is so familiar today. The red

From left: The Original Protegimus; The new team
'Protegimus'; One of the corporate 'Protegimus'

plume was chosen as it represented the Corps well, the red cap (later beret), stable belt, arm band, red stripe down the leg of No 1 dress and the 'Robin Red Breasted' tabard worn by SNCOs and Officers under mess jackets. The red plume also stood out from a variety of backgrounds. Capt Allwood supported the motto and after approval by the Provost Marshal, Sgt Glover made a trip to Belfast and a gentleman's outfitters of some renown and a few weeks later the first batch of 50 'CP' ties were produced. The ties were then awarded to members of 177 upon their departure (and were a welcome replacement to the traditional tankard!). The motif remained unchanged until 2007, when it was brought up-to-date to reflect the corporate image of the CPU.

Chapter 11
The Team Photograph

As anyone with an understanding of the military will know, tradition born many years ago forms much of a unit's or regiment's identity today. One such tradition within RMP Close Protection is the team photograph. Taken once during the tour with the principal, and sometimes with family members, every team will have a photo taken and if a particular post is ongoing teams will always try and out-do the photo before, having the picture taken in the most interesting and often obscure places possible. Within the lounge of Kitchener House over 150 team photographs adorn the walls and range from the one taken in Beirut in 1983 through a military team posing on the Cross Swords[1] in Baghdad, to the top of the historic wall that tops the mountains surrounding Kabul in Afghanistan. No matter what size the team, a photo with the 'Boss' always arrived at Longmoor and found its place on the lounge wall. There is even one with the Chargé d'Affaires, Alistair Newton, with his two bodyguards, who all spent a few months in Bujumbura, Burundi on the northern shores of Lake Tanganyika. Although military photos have now joined the collection in Kitchener House, what are not shown within the lounge are the pre-FCO photos, of which there are many. The relationship between military commanders and their teams are such that photos with the 'General' were, relatively speaking, common place. Whether the photos were taken outside HQNI in Northern Ireland 40 years ago or in the Ambassador's garden in Khartoum (with Cpl (later Capt) Taff Pike in 1992 or SSgt Keightley in 2007), they are all a small snapshot of history themselves and as long as RMP CP teams continue to deploy, the 'photo archive' will continue to grow within Kitchener House.

---

1   The Swords of Qādisīyah, also called the Crossed Swords, are a pair of triumphal arches in central Baghdad, Iraq and were constructed to commemorate the then Iraqi President Saddam Hussein's declaration of victory over Iran in the Iran-Iraq war (though the war was considered by many to have ended in stalemate).

THE TEAM PHOTOGRAPH   187

Right to Left: Sgt Benton RMP, Cpl C Carnall RMP, Capt Farrar-Hockley, Maj Gen Farrar-Hockley CLF, Cpl 'Porky' Watson, (then names unknown) Northern Ireland 1970.

ROYAL MILITARY POLICE CLOSE PROTECTION TEAM
FCO KAMPALA DECEMBER 1988-JUNE 1989
CPL IAN FARRIN, CPL EDDIE HALL, SSGT TOM WALSH, JOSEPH (BHC DVR), SGT MARK SLATER,
CPL KIRK DAVIES, CPL STEVE HODSON

ROYAL MILITARY POLICE CLOSE PROTECTION TEAM
BFCME OP GRANBY
OCTOBER 1990 - MARCH 1991

Rear Rank: Cpl I M Robinson RM, Sgt P D Irvine RMP, Cpl K J Bulman RMP, Cpl I Cameron RMP, Cpl S J Levick RMP, Sgt A T Cain RCT.
Front Rank: SSgt C J Young RMP, Cdr C D Ferbrache OBE, RN, Lt Gen Sir Peter De La Billiere KCB, CBE, DSO, MC, Maj J M Chapman LI, Sgt D R Green RMP

THE TEAM PHOTOGRAPH

ROYAL MILITARY POLICE CLOSE PROTECTION TEAM
MOSTAR 2/97

CA Gwinnell TS Hardaker
KRE Lennox SA Ellison
Sir Martin Garrod KCB OBE

ROYAL MILITARY POLICE CLOSE PROTECTION TEAM
DCG MNF (I)
Feb – Sept 2006

Capt Tom Simpson ADC, LT Gen Rob Fry DCG,

Sgt Paul Andrews, LCpl Lee Simpson, Lt Col Graham Cundy MA, SSgt Richard Keightley

Cpl Nathan Chapman, Sgt Karl Shone, Maj Jon Lauer USADC, Cpl 'Taff' Clark

ROYAL MILITARY POLICE HIGH READINESS TEAM
KHARTOUM
September – December 2007
Sgt Paul Burton, Cpl Jon Ashley, Sgt 'Burt' Reynolds.
Sgt Lloyd Paterson, HMA Dr Rosalind Marsden, SSgt Richard Keightley.
George

Chapter 12

Behind the Scenes

Any military operation conducted by an army will fail without the support of its logisticians – those men and women responsible for the resupply of front line troops with ammunition, rations, vehicle spares and specialist equipment that is necessary to ensure the success of the mission. During World War 2, Sgt George Whiting CMP, escorting Field Marshal Montgomery, would have been equipped by the same logistic chain that catered for his comrades, who were conducting duties as military policemen but as the importance of escort duties became more apparent, those appointed to undertake those duties recognised that the kit and equipment supplied was no longer fit for purpose. As such, close protection operators, certainly in the early days of the 'troubles' in Northern Ireland, would often deploy with various weapons and equipment that they in turn adapted to their own personal taste. The NCO would no doubt be at the top of his game and confident that his weapons were some of the best that could have been issued to a member of the RMP. However, it would have caused headaches for the Quartermaster responsible for 177 (Sp) Coy. Maintaining an equipment account is difficult enough without having to contend with individuals, who, due to the mechanics of the day, wanted different things in order to afford the protection to the principals for which they were responsible. This practice continued until the formation of the Operations Wing at Longmoor and the appointment of Lt. Col (Retired) Steve Manning OBE as the first 'CP' Regimental Admin Officer. In addition to his duties as admin officer, (responsible for the deployment of teams, finances, flights and diplomatic relations), Lt Col Manning also managed the equipment account for teams deployed abroad and permanent staff at home.

All vehicles, weapons and equipment were purchased by the FCO and it wasn't long until the Heckler and Koch (HK) weapon systems were introduced. Whether an HK was 9mm, 5.56mm or 7.62mm, the operation of each was the same. The pistol of choice, the 9mm Browning Hi Power, had been introduced earlier but now, at last, CP operators were issued with standard weapons across the board, albeit far removed from their RMP colleagues who were still using

Examples of Courier Passports issued to members of CP teams to maximize the opportunity to deliver diplomatic mail to the Embassy.

Armoured Toyota Land Cruiser. Being similar to its civilian counterpart the 'discreet' Land Cruiser is the preferred vehicle of choice for many Close Protection teams operating in hostile environments (this one is pictured in Khartoum).

the Sterling SMG and unwieldy 7.62mm SLR.

All deployment of personnel and equipment was paid for by the FCO and the rules governing the budget was determined following a request to DMO for team deployment. For example, during the first Gulf War, five extra teams were trained, equipped and deployed within 10 days. A Service Level Agreement between the MOD and the FCO was established and the CP mission moved forward with considerable speed with the migration of equipment to the CP operations being conducted in Northern Ireland and Germany bringing unity to the RMP CP mission globally. Between 1981 and 2011, over 300 teams have deployed in support of the FCO and MOD, but, until 1997, the Operations Wing did not even have a Quartermaster, 'just' an RAO and a JNCO appointed to assist. There is a continuing mantra within CPU that the mission comes first and to that end the teams required kit replacements and the introduction of new equipment. It often fell upon the shoulders of a sole JNCO armed with nothing but a Couriers Passport and a bag full of luck to deliver whatever it was that the team required. Much wrangling between Longmoor and the FCO meant the teams did not go wanting. Capt (Ret'd) Paul Allan took on the mantle from Lt Col Manning and it was in 1997 that SSgt Vince Barrett RMP was appointed as the first Company Quartermaster to the RMP Operations Wing ably assisted by Cpl 'Flash' Hannan. Both were trained Close Protection operators and had deployed on CP duties previously so had an understanding of the demands that were made by teams abroad and the basis for those demands. As the operation increased in size the equipment account was worth millions of pounds and with that growth the need for an accomplished G4[1] department became apparent. By 2000, operations were supported by an appointed Quartermaster, who was also the second-in-command of the unit, a Regimental Quartermaster Sergeant, a CQMS, a Motor Transport (MT) SNCO, a REME Sgt Armourer, a JNCO ammunition storeman, an MT JNCO and a civilian storeman as well as support within the Foreign and Commonwealth Office.

The Close Protection Warrant Officer is responsible for appointing individuals to teams from all branches of the service police as well as attached drivers from any quarter of the army. An Ops Officer, Ops Warrant Officer and Ops Clerk manage those teams that are deployed on operations and with a combined staff of over 100 personnel, administration is managed by an RAO,

---

1 G4 – Army organisation is subdivided into categories G1 – 9 each representing a different component of the command structure. G4 is that which caters for logistics and quartering.

a Chief Clerk, and a Clerk, with additional support provided by HQ SEME in Bordon. It is very easy to focus on the excitement that guns, bullets, nice cars and helicopters present but without the behind-the-scenes efforts of modern-day logisticians within the G4 department, CP teams would not even leave Longmoor.

On the 21st November 2012, at about nine in the morning, the true value of the kit and equipment issued to Close Protection teams was tested to the full when an armoured Land Cruiser was attacked in Kabul. WO2 Paul 'Shep' Shephard MBE RMP was visiting the RMP teams in Kabul as part of an OPEVAL in his capacity as Operations Warrant Officer at Longmoor. WO2 Shephard was travelling through what was known as 'the Green Zone' (a semi-porous security bubble that was home to much of the Military and Political command as well as the diplomatic quarter) with Cpl Smith RMP and the driver LCpl Gillott 17 Port Maritime, who had deployed to Kabul in support of operations. Approximately 150m south of the British Embassy and 200m from HQ ISAF, approaching a vehicle checkpoint, traffic was at a virtual standstill. WO2 Shephard sat in the rear right of the vehicle when a man dressed in local clothing was challenged by the guard at the checkpoint as he was deemed suspicious. Standing at the roadside about 3m from WO2 Shephard and 2m in front of a wall, the man detonated an IED he was wearing killing himself and four others. Luckily for the survivors, the suicide bomber also killed a second bomber before he could detonate his own device.

There were a number of vehicles that were very badly damaged. The Land Cruiser the team were travelling in sustained damage to the engine bay and all four tyres were punctured. Later it was established that the device contained 5-7kg of military grade explosive that had 1000s of ball bearings packed tightly around it contained in AK47 type magazine pouches. It was reported that this was the first time such high grade explosives had been used.

With the engine bay billowing smoke and body parts and blood obscuring the windows making visibility difficult, WO2 Shephard took charge and ordered the driver to get the vehicle away as quickly as possible, only slowing when they reached the relative safety of the American checkpoint, the run-flat tyres doing their job. On entering HQ ISAF, the vehicle was parked. The damage can be clearly seen and on getting out, WO2 Shephard saw what appeared to be an ear stuck to his door. Taking off his body armour, WO2 Shephard went to his next meeting, apologising in true British fashion for being late.

BEHIND THE SCENES 195

The explosives removed from the second suicide bomber.

The damage caused to the wall by the detonation of the first device by the suicide bomber who was standing approximately 2m in front of it.

The Toyota Land Cruiser with flat tyres, damaged windows and holes where the ball bearings struck. The integrity of the armour was not compromised.

Chapter 13
A CP Operator Always Looks Out

For quite some time the Army have adopted a motto similar to 'Join the Army, see the World'. Although not entirely accurate, it may be argued that on joining the British Army nowadays a serviceman will generally only see Afghanistan, Poland, Northern Ireland or Germany. RMP CP operators are no exception, often deploying on exercise or real-time operations to any of the mainstream theatres in support of General Police Duties. In addition to these, individuals have also had the opportunity to travel to some of the most dangerous, isolated areas on earth. Notwithstanding the obvious hardships that hostile environments present, no matter where a serviceman or -woman may serve, there are still things to see, people to meet, friends to make and memories to cherish. This closing chapter is an attempt to capture some of those memories from CP operators past and present showing that they do indeed always looks out, and what they would miss if they didn't.

Embassy Vehicle Car Wash, Sierra Leone taken by WO1 (RSM) Neil Ashton in 2001.

198 DETER SUPPRESS EXTRACT!

The photo above shows the beauty and majesty of Rwanda. The photo below shows refugees returning to Rwanda following the genocide resulting in the deaths of thousands of men, women and children.

Even with nothing, these Rwandan children were happy to come home. Many children throughout the Hutu-Tutsi war were maimed by the opposing tribe making life extremely difficult for the families and orphanages that cared for them.

The Roman ruins at Baalbek in the Bekaa Valley in Lebanon are some of the finest examples of Roman architecture found today although it is reported that some of the ruins predate the Romans by approximately 2000 years. Baalbek also means 'City of the Sun'.

SSgt Lloyd Paterson sailing on the River Nile with the British Ambassador in Sudan. You can just make out the butt of a C8 rifle and radio antenna within the PES speed boat.

A taxi ride in Khartoum.

SSgt Lloyd Paterson RMP enjoying lunch in the shade whilst exploring the deserts of Sudan with the Deputy Head of Mission, British Embassy, Khartoum.

A Dinka tribesman showing the markings of the tribe, seen here in Juba, southern Sudan (later Republic of South Sudan).

Baghdad skyline taken from a Blackhawk helicopter.

Sgt Paul Andrews Royal Marines, Close Protection Team driver, manning the Minimi Light Machine Gun as an Apache helicopter provides top cover in Northern Iraq.

A CP OPERATOR ALWAYS LOOKS OUT 203

Following the devastation in Haiti, a burst water main was the closest thing to a shower its town's people had for a very long time.

The Hindu Kush mountain range in central Afghanistan taken during a road move with the Principal.

Maj Gen James Bucknall Chief of Staff International Security Assistance Force with his Bodyguard, Cpl Andy Cooper RMP and MA on the medieval wall overlooking Kabul which proved a popular form of exercise for Ambassadors and military commanders alike.

The wall in winter.

Kabul on fire, viewed from 'TV Hill'.

A game of Buzkashi being played north of Kabul. The photograph was taken by the British Ambassador, Sir Sherard Cowper-Coles KCMG CMG LVO, with the CP team close by.

206   DETER SUPPRESS EXTRACT!

Whether collecting firewood or throwing a clay pot, daily life in Afghanistan continues despite the troubles incumbent with conflict.

A CP OPERATOR ALWAYS LOOKS OUT

Images of Afghanistan taken by members of the Close Protection Team, British Embassy Kabul 2003.

A tribesman in Ethiopia taken by Cpl Steve Gray RMP whilst delivering specialist training to local law enforcement.

208 **DETER SUPPRESS EXTRACT!**

Images of Afghanistan taken by members of the Close Protection Team, British Embassy Kabul 2003.

A view along the Panjshir Valley taken whilst the British Ambassador visited the area and its Governor.

Cpl Fraser Dyer RMP whilst on patrol in Kandahar City, Afghanistan.

Whilst in Baghdad the Principal and CP team would often join American callsigns on patrols. Here they can be seen entering a Forward Operating Base in the north of the city.

SSgt (now Capt) Sean Kimber RMP standing between two Dragon Blood trees which are a distinctive and slow-growing species native to the Socotra archipelago off the horn of Africa.

A CP OPERATOR ALWAYS LOOKS OUT

Local Yemeni males walking through a small village near Sana'a with their AKM assault rifles. It is believed they were to provide the celebratory fire at a local wedding.

Epilogue

Brigadier E.O. Forster-Knight CBE
Former Provost Marshal (Army)

This book is about the people that have gone before us as military policemen and women serving their country at home and overseas. It has described the transformation of the traditional military police 'escort' role through to what is now the deployment of highly professional and well-equipped Royal Military Police Close Protection Teams to high threat environments across the World supporting both Her Majesty's Ambassadors and High Commissioners and senior military commanders. It is a record of sustained devotion to duty and professionalism of which we can all be rightly proud.

The Royal Military Police continues to set the standards for Close Protection operations across the world. In 2011, Royal Military Police personnel are engaged in some 16 operational deployments across the Globe, in countries ranging from South America to South East Asia. The dedication, shown by those before us, continues on a daily basis.

Exemplo Ducemus

It has been an adventure so far, long may it continue

Appendix I
The Protegimus Grace

Dear Lord we thank you for the food we are
about to eat in the company of friends.

We ask you to bless the people here present, those deployed
on operations and our absent CP colleagues.

We remember in our prayers all CP operators throughout
the world as they endeavour to protect others.

We ask you to make them steadfast, loyal, patient, and
determined. May they act decisively and with skill when
called upon to react; never lacking courage or honour.

Make them courteous – always remembering they have a
responsibility to lead by example and with humility.

Amen

Appendix II

Appointments, Honours and Awards

Close Protection Officer BAOR

Maj NC Crew	1977-1979
Maj PE Townsend MBE	1981-1983
Capt KT Bacon	1984-1985
Capt PK Williams MM	1985-1986

Special Operations Officer RMP BAOR

Maj KT Bacon MBE	Feb 1987-Jul 1990
Maj SG Hayes	Jul 1990-Nov 1991
Maj JC Dawson	Nov 1991-May 1992
Maj RM Moore	Jan 1993-Mar 1994

Close Protection Team Special Operations Wing RMP Germany

Capt JD Tasker	Apr 1994-Apr 1995
Capt DA Smith	Apr 1998-Apr 2000

Warrant Officer Close Protection Team (Germany)

WO2 EU Grant	Jan 1984-Jul 1986
WO2 D Jones	Jul 1986-Apr 1987
WO2 TJ Plank	Apr 1987-Sep 1988
WO2 SR Hardaker	Sep 1988-Jun 1992
WO2 HA Roberts	Jun 1992-Oct 1994
WO2 BR Barnes	Oct 1994-Dec 1997
WO2 D McNeill	Dec 1997-Mar 1998
WO2 SM Smith	Mar 1998-Mar 1999
WO2 DR Thomas	Mar 1999-Apr 2000
WO2 MJ Jackson	Apr 2000-Jun 2001
WO2 AJ Pike	Jun 2001-Feb 2002

Close Protection Team Germany Team Leader

Cpl CE Jones	Apr 2002-Sep 2002
Sgt SS Henderson Reid	Sep 2002-Sep 2003
Sgt DG Deacon	Sep 2003-Sep 2004
Sgt N Cowen	Sep 2004-Mar 2005
Sgt GS Hannan	Mar 2005

Officer Commanding RMP Operations Wing Longmoor

Maj Colin Watkins	Circa 1979
Maj Ken Greenland	1982-1987
Maj AP Collins	Sep 1987-Aug 1990
Maj GL Powell	Sep 1990-Oct 1992
Maj IAR Stenning MBE	Nov 1992-Sep 1994
Maj KJ Blake BEM	Oct 1994-Jun 1995
Maj JT Green	Jul 1995-Mar 1996

Officer Commanding Close Protection Unit RMP

Maj JT Green	Apr 1996-Mar 1998
Maj MC Bottomley BEM	Apr 1998-Feb 2001
Maj S Dorset	Feb 2001-Aug 2003
Maj PSMA Cairns	Aug 2003-Jun 2006
Maj J Watson	Jun 2006-May 2007
Maj PF Wellington MBE	May 2007-Feb 2009
Maj AM Banks	Feb 2009-Jan 2012
Maj M John	Jan 2012-

Close Protection Unit Warrant Officer

WO1 HA Roberts	Oct 1995-Apr 1998
WO1 D McNeill	Apr 1998-May 2000
WO1 CJ Young	May 2000-Mar 2002
WO1 N Shufflebottom	Mar 2002-Apr 2004
WO1 GR Keighley	Apr 2004-Oct 2006
WO1 MJ Marley	Oct 2006-Apr 2008
WO1 MD Lycett	Apr 2008-May 2010
WO1 NA Ashton	May 2010-

Officer Commanding 177 Support Company

Capt Brian Wood	1971-1973
Capt John Allwood	1973-1974
Capt Artur Liver	1974-1976
Capt Ian Fulton	1978-1980
Capt Mike Ayling	1980

Company Sergeant Major 177 Support Company

SSgt Carroll	1972-1973
WO2 O'Donnell	1978-1980
WO2 Harding	1980

39 Brigade Provost Unit & 177 (Support) Platoon Officer Commanding

Lt Allan Cray	1986-1987
Capt Ken Blake BEM	1987-1990
Capt Mick Bottomley BEM	1990-
Capt HR Shepherd	Jun 1997-Jun 1999
Capt PF Wellington	Jun 1999-May 2000

39 Brigade Provost Unit & 177 (Support) Platoon Company Sergeant Major

WO2 (CSM) McDonald	1987-
WO2 (CSM) Kerridge	
WO2 (CSM) S Webster	Jun 1997-Aug 1997
WO2 (CSM) MS Sandiford	Aug 1997-Mar 1999

Close Protection Warrant Officer Northern Ireland

WO2 RW Newman	Jun 2000-

Officer in Charge 177 (Support) Platoon

Capt MR Bird	May 2000-Aug 2001
Capt MC Osborne	Aug 2001-Apr 2002
Capt DR Thomas MBE	May 2002-Apr 2003
Capt M Pickford	May 2003-Sep 2004
Capt L Neal	Sep 2004-Aug 2005
Maj DM Gartland	Aug 2005-Jan 2006
Maj MR Bird	Jan 2006-Aug 2006

APPOINTMENTS, HONOURS AND AWARDS

RMP Operations Wing Honours and Awards

SSgt Blake K	CP Operations	BEM 1980
SSgt Laffan	CPTL Kampala	QGM 1982
Cpl Gerrard	CPT Kampala	QCBC 1982
Cpl Rodgers KD	CPT Beirut	BEM 1985
SSgt Mudd AK	CPTL Beirut	BEM 1989
SSgt Hemmingway JR	CPTL Beirut	BEM 1990
SSgt Jones RM	CPTL Beirut	BEM 1991
SSgt Moon VH	CPTL Beirut	BEM 1991
SSgt Fahrenholz PR	CPTL Bogota	BEM 1991
Maj AP Collins	OC Ops Wing	MBE 1991
SSgt Ball P	CPTL Doha	BEM 1992
SSgt Watson BR	CPTL Beirut	BEM 1992
SSgt Dobson OJ	CPTL Beirut	BEM 1993
SSgt Levick SJ	CPTL Algiers	MBE 1997
SSgt Richards JJ	CPTL Algiers	MBE 1997
SSgt Cooper AR	CPTL Algiers	MBE 1997
Sgt Scott RMS	CPTL Freetown	QCVS 1999
SSgt Thomas DR	CPTL Freetown	MBE 2000
Capt PF Wellington	CPTL Kabul	MBE 2003
Sgt Powell RJ	CPT Kabul	MBE 2003
Lt Col S Dorset	OC CPU RMP	MBE 2004
Sgt Shepherd PJ	CP Operations	MBE 2006

Bibliography

Arthur, Max, "General Tuzo", *The Independent* [Obituaries] (19 August 1998)

Dibbens, Harold, *Dibbens' Diaries as a Sailor, Soldier, Policeman, Civil Servant* (Self Published 1989)

Edgar, Elaine, *A Journey Between Souls* (White-Boucke Publishing 1997)

Geraghty, Tony, *The Bullet Catchers* (Grafton 1989)

ISAF Website, Key Facts and Figures at http://www.isaf.nato.int/images/stories/File/2013-12-01%20ISAF%20Placemat-final.pdf

Knowles, Mike, *Protection Squad* (Issue 2712) *Commando* © D.C. Thomson & Co Ltd (November 1993)

Lovell-Knight, A.V., *The Story of the Royal Military Police* (Leo Cooper 1977)

Mander, Danny, *Winston Churchill's Bodyguard* (MMSolutions 11 November 2002)

Pidd, Helen, "Remains of British journalist Alec Collett found in Lebanon", *Guardian Online* (23 November 2009) at http://www.guardian.co.uk/media/2009/nov/23/alec-collett-remains-found-lebanon

RMP Corps Journal Second Quarter (1952)

RMP Corps Journal Third Quarter (1998)

RMP Corps Journal Third Quarter (1999)

RMP Corps Journal Fourth Quarter (1999)

RMP Corps Journal Second Quarter (2005)

RMP Corps Journal Third Quarter (2005)

RMP Corps Journal Fourth Quarter (2008)

Turnbull, JD SSgt, *The Ulster Watchdogs 1969-1974* (Publisher Unknown 1975)

Turnbull, JD SSgt, *The Ulster Watchdogs 1974-1984* (Publisher Unknown 1984)

Various, *Operation Banner – An Analysis of Military Operations in Northern Ireland* (Crown Publishing 2006)

Unknown, "British journalist McCarthy kidnapped", BBC Online 'On this day in history' (17 April 1986) at http://news.bbc.co.uk/onthisday/hi/dates/stories/april/17/newsid_4693000/4693188.stm

Unknown, "Beirut hostage John McCarthy freed", BBC Online 'On this day in history' (8 August 1991) at http://news.bbc.co.uk/onthisday/hi/dates/stories/august/8/newsid_2492000/2492499.stm

Wikipedia *Alfredo Ignacio Astiz* (updated 19 March 13) at http://en.wikipedia.org/wiki/Alfredo_Astiz